THE GRA[...]
IN THE [...]

John Cheeseman
Philip Gardner
Michael Sadgrove
Tom Wright

THE BANNER OF TRUTH TRUST

THE BANNER OF TRUTH TRUST
3 Murrayfield Road, Edinburgh EH12 6EL
PO Box 621, Carlisle, Pennsylvania 17013, USA

*

© John Cheeseman, Philip Gardner,
Michael Sadgrove, Tom Wright

First published 1972
Reprinted 1976

ISBN 0 85151 153 8

*

Set in 11-12 pt Walbaum
and printed in Great Britain by
Hazell Watson & Viney Ltd
Aylesbury, Bucks

Preface

A few words concerning the circumstances in which this book came to be written may be appropriate. The work is the fruit, not of abstract speculation, but of discussions that took place in the context of the day-to-day life of the Oxford Inter-Collegiate Christian Union. At the time when much of this book was written, the four of us were members of the Executive Committee of the Union, and our particular concerns were for the corporate life of the Christian Union, as a fellowship of believers in the Lord Jesus Christ, and for the presentation of the Gospel to members of the University. Our writing was motivated by practical considerations, far removed from idle theorizing or disputing about words; our single desire being the greater glory of Almighty God in the life of our Union. Our prayer was, and is, that the watchword *Soli Deo Gloria* should crown all that we do in testifying to the Gospel of the grace of God. We wrote the book as undergraduates, and it gives evidence, no doubt, of undergraduate immaturity. We would ask, therefore, that what we have written be judged, not according to unfortunate modes of expression or unevenness of style, but simply according to the Holy Scriptures, the sole court of appeal by which all that we say stands or falls. We shall almost certainly be criticized for writing this — by some for writing it at all, by some for being too doctrinaire and extremist, by others, possibly, for not going far enough. We apologize in advance for our immature understanding, judgement, and powers of expression, and for any sweeping criticisms, seemingly lacking in love, which we have never intended, but which some may see in these pages. We do not apologize for the work as a whole, for we would not have undertaken it had we not been convinced that God intended us to do so.

If the highest moral good were the maintenance of a *status quo*, this book would not have been written. We are well aware that there are things contained in it with which many whom we respect and admire would disagree. We know that we are opposing certain views held dear by many a firm Christian: we realize that some will be wary of the sort of things we say, knowing that in the past unscriptural views have been based upon similar teaching, with disastrous results. We must say at the outset, therefore, that we in no way want to appear to be lecturing our elders and betters: that, rather, we hope to state seriously views which we believe are Biblical; that we hope that we are alive to all the possible dangers that will be foreseen by others, and that we have taken steps to note and correct them. It is well known that in the past there have been those who, starting from Biblical doctrine, have constructed logical superstructures over and above what the Bible actually says, killing evangelism on the one hand, or minimizing their view of God on the other. We hope and pray – and try to show – that what we have said is directly Biblical. We would say from the start that we believe strongly in the majesty and sovereignty of God *and* in the clear Scriptural commands to preach the Gospel; and we would ask any who disagree with us to do so, not on the grounds of what they think we may imply, but of what we actually say.

In conclusion, we should like to thank several friends for their helpful and constructive criticism of our work; in particular, the Banner of Truth Trust, for the warm and encouraging interest they have shown. Our prayer is that the Lord God of Israel, who has visited and redeemed his people, may, through the eternal truths of the Gospel presented in this book, be uplifted, glorified and worshipped in the hearts of all who shall read it.

JOHN CHEESEMAN *Oriel College*
PHILIP GARDNER *Jesus College*
MICHAEL SADGROVE *Balliol College*
TOM WRIGHT *Exeter College*

Oxford, September 1971

Note
Biblical quotations have been taken mainly from the Authorized Version and the Revised Version, and also occasionally from the Revised Standard Version.

Contents

INTRODUCTION

'Of making many books there is no end, and much study is a weariness of the flesh.' With the Preacher's words to remind us, as though we might have forgotten, we write not in order to have written something, nor in order to please anyone, nor because we particularly enjoy writing for its own sake. This book is produced, rather, as a result of firmly held convictions, and of deep concern and alarm at various things that are being taught and practised to-day. Our aim is simple: to present and expound what we believe are the basic truths of the Christian Gospel, to demonstrate these from the teaching of Scripture, and to show, in some measure, some ways in which they are currently being diverted and misapplied – not from a desire to score points off fellow-Christians, nor for the sake of fanning theological fires, but rather from a reluct-ant but determined desire to re-assert truth that is in danger of being lost – and then to apply this truth to prac-tical Christian living. Our aim in charting rocks and shal-lows is not a perverse delight in them for their own sake, but so that ships may have a safe voyage.

In case it should be thought that, despite the above claims, we are indulging in polemic with no good reason, it may help if we outline briefly the reasons why we have undertaken this task. They are basically two: one theological and the other practical. The first is obviously the stronger, and would stand without the second, which, however, corroborates and supports it helpfully.

First, the theological reason. It has been said that

whereas evangelicals in the 1890's talked of being 'saved', by the 1930's they spoke of being 'converted', and today they talk of being 'committed'. That this is neither a trivial linguistic phenomenon nor a petty quibbling-point can easily be seen in the light of an examination of why this shift has occurred. The implications behind the three words illustrate well our whole point. 'Saved' conveys the idea of man being rescued from some sort of desperate plight. This salvation includes conversion and commitment, but is not reducible to the terms of either or both. 'Converted' recognizes the need for a man to be born again, and includes commitment; but the idea of being saved from wrath, from the consequences of sin, has been lost in a polite re-wording of such offensive but thoroughly Biblical truth. The present-day 'committed', to be found in such phrases as 'I committed myself', 'becoming fully committed', 'made an initial step of commitment', and the like, is the product of a much more radical change of thought, which has not only lost sight of the basic life-and-death issues involved when a man is born again, and brought out of darkness into light, but also made the action and its effects the operations of man. The subject of the verb 'committed' is man: that of 'saved' is indubitably God.

We would not be so foolish as to suggest that all who use the word 'commit' accept the implication which we have just stated. But we believe that this linguistic slide is symptomatic of, and gives us a clue to, a fundamental inversion of the Gospel which is the cause of much current error. Basically, we are convinced that some present teaching in the Christian world has put the emphasis on man and his needs, his fulfilment, his commitment, his responsibility and opportunity. Without denying at all that man has needs, one of which is fulfilment, or that he needs to be committed to Christ, or that he is a responsible creature with opportunities before him, we think that such a presentation is worse than a half-truth, and indeed is positively misleading, in that it has left out of the picture the Lord God who not only made man in the first place, but also is the active agent in the salvation of a soul. This is our basic reason for writing as we do: our work will consist of an examination in detail of what this involves.

The second reason, the practical one, is easily seen by examining current difficulties and points of weakness in our Christian community, and by noticing the uncanny way in which they are traceable either completely or in part to teaching of this modern and man-centred type. Not that we are presenting an instant one-step cure-all: perfection is as far away as man's nature is evil. But recognition of the root cause of a problem must be the first step towards a cure: and the symptoms of the problem are not far off. Our prayers need to be stimulated by reminders of what needs to be prayed for. Our love for the Scriptures is so shallow that we are content to skimp a passage like a careless lamb playing in a field when a wise sheep would be taking nourishment! We have no thirst to hear the Word preached, and in consequence some have given up expounding it, for want of willing hearers. And – who can be surprised? – we have lost the vision for souls that characterized the days when men talked of being 'saved' and meant it.

This has affected alike our missionary outlook and our ordinary evangelistic outreach. Would any of this be so, if we all had the definite and thrilling knowledge that the Lord God himself had chosen and called us, without our deserving it, out of the darkness and complete deadness of sin – had forgiven us freely, and was going to give us, through Christ, an eternal weight of glory – and had given us, now and here, the Holy Spirit to live in us? Or what if this, which is no doubt head-knowledge for most of us, became heart-knowledge – burnt into us so that we could not forget it? Would not then our prayer be with gratitude and joy? Would we not be so filled with amazement and thanks for his love that we would willingly go anywhere and do anything for him? Would not our approach to the Bible be with eager reverence, delighting to be taught by it? Would we not gladly go into all the world – the next-door house or room, as well as the ends of the earth – to tell men and women of the incredible mercy and love of the Lord? But we do not – and it is hardly surprising. For instead of the mercy of God we are used to thinking of the 'need for commitment'. Instead of salvation from sin and destruction we search for peace of mind and fulfilment. Adam sinned by desiring to be 'as God'; but we are in danger of estimating ourselves to be *more* important than God – and this is undoubtedly having its effect. Our experience, limited though it is, suggests that this point is a vital one for present-day Christians.

The Church is, at the time of writing, much given to talk of unity. We, believing that there can be no real unity without truth as a basic presupposition, would also wish to draw attention to the fact that it has been at times when men have re-examined and re-experienced the basic doctrines of the Bible that the Church has taken great steps forward: and, conversely, when anything but the revealed truth of God as it stands in Scripture has been the foundation, heresy and division have rotted the whole building. We therefore present what we have to say, to any who care to study it, in the hope that it will play some part, whether large or small, in bringing the Church, the company of regenerate men and women, more into line with what God has revealed in his Word. It is our hope and earnest prayer that this will result, by the working of his Spirit, in great glory to his Name in the devotion of grateful Christians, and in the salvation of many.

Finally, some remarks on what this book is not. It is not a manual of theology, giving a full and systematic account of what the Bible teaches. Nor is it a personal credo, or a compilation of personal credos. Nor is it a blueprint for a successful Christian organization or life. To hope to achieve any such ends would be futile: each community must learn to live in the light of the Word alone if it is to live as God wants it to. Nor are we pretending to have 'discovered' a new doctrine, or a new emphasis of doctrine, which has either been revealed to us specifically, or upon which we, by some fluke or miracle, have stumbled. We merely wish to restate a very old, well-formulated doctrine, which finds expression, for instance, in the 39 Articles and the Westminster Confession (as well as in such brief statements as the IVF Basis of Faith). So we are not, we trust, saying anything new: it would alarm us if we thought we were. We are, rather, giving voice to a truth which has been silent in some quarters for some time, and whose absence has been, we feel, the indirect and direct cause of much that is at fault in our Christian teaching and practice.

We therefore hope simply to turn men's eyes back to what the Bible teaches, and gently to suggest ways of current application. The latter will, of course, be limited by the circumstances which we know, whereas the former is there for all to see, and stands by itself. We will follow the example of St. Paul in first setting out doctrine, and then turning to practical applications. This book is about the Gospel, God's Gospel of grace: and so we shall begin by asking some basic questions about this Gospel, and examining its fundamental points.

At the end of each chapter we have added some questions which might be voiced by someone who disagrees, or who has doubts about what we have said; and we have attempted briefly to answer each question, without intending to be exhaustive or determinative.

1

BIBLICAL FOUNDATIONS:
GOD AND MAN

We say again what was affirmed above: our aim throughout this book, but pre-eminently in these initial chapters,
is to find out what Scripture teaches, and to plead for
heartfelt and unconditional acceptance of those doctrines
which the Holy Spirit has sealed with his authority in his
inspiration of God's infallible and inerrant Word. The
'faith once delivered to the saints', for which we are commanded to contend *earnestly*,[1] is that teaching which the
Lord Jesus Christ left with his apostles; that doctrine in
which the young Church continued; that doctrine, the
possession of which is one of the marks of a truly apostolic
Church. It is this doctrine, and no other, which we shall
attempt to set forth in these chapters.

We believe that nothing less than the full truth of the
great doctrines of grace, is the Gospel of Holy Scripture. It
hardly matters whether this theology is termed Calvinistic, Augustinian or Reformed, since any system of divinity
stands or falls according as it is, or is not, thoroughly Scrip-
ture-based, and in harmony with the entire content of
God's Holy Word. Spurgeon's words will bear repetition:

'The old truth that Calvin preached, that Augustine
preached, that Paul preached, is the truth that I must
preach today, or else be false to my conscience and my
God. I cannot shape the truth; I know of no such thing as
paring off the rough edges of a doctrine. John Knox's
Gospel is my Gospel. That which thundered through
Scotland must thunder through England again.'

1. Jude 3

To the question, 'What is the Christian Gospel?', Martin Luther gives an admirable answer:

'*Evangel* is a Greek word, meaning glad tidings, good news, welcome information, a shout, or something that makes one sing, talk or rejoice. When David defeated the giant Goliath, there was a great shout, and an encouraging message was passed round among the Jews to say that their terrible enemy had been killed, and that they were free to enjoy liberty and peace; thereupon, they sang and danced, and made merry. Similarly, God's evangel, the New Testament, is a good piece of news, a war-cry. It was echoed throughout the world by the apostles. They proclaimed a true David, who had done combat with, and gained the victory over, sin, death, and the devil. In so doing, he had taken those who were enchained by sin, threatened by death, and overpowered by the devil; though they had merited no rewards, he redeemed them, justified them, gave them life and salvation, and so brought them peace, and led them back to God.'

This Gospel, the Evangel, which *evangelicals* love to proclaim, is a message which tells of One who turns rebels into worshippers; 'a proclamation of divine sovereignty in mercy and judgement, a summons to bow down and worship the mighty Lord on whom man depends for all good, both in nature, and grace.' The Gospel tells of the glorious triumph of God's life-giving free GRACE that saves, over the will of man that leads to his condemnation and death; this grace is that free and unmerited favour of God toward sinners, by which God the Father loved us and had mercy upon us; by which the Lord Jesus Christ came to earth to die for our sins; and by which the Holy Spirit called us and drew us out of darkness into God's marvellous light. This is indeed good news; it is the very kernel of the 'whole counsel of God'[2] which Paul and the rest of the apostles did not shrink from declaring, proclaiming to the world the great work of the three persons of the Trinity in saving sinners.

God

The Gospel begins where the Bible begins, and where all true religion begins – with God himself. The Gospel is God's Gospel; it is his power; it tells of his righteousness, his grace and his truth.[3] In short, the Gospel is about God. Whenever superficiality, glibness, frivolity, stereotyped evangelism, and suchlike, abound, while reverence, depth, personal desire for holiness, and overflowing love for the Lord Jesus are not very obvious, we may be certain that the root cause of the trouble is that the gospel that is preached is not the God-centred Biblical Gospel, but a new, man-made, man-centred substitute, such as the Galatians sought after. The Gospel we find in the Bible is concerned with God; it seeks to glorify him, and him alone. This Gospel causes men to fear God, love God, and glorify God; and any gospel which does not do these things is not the Gospel which the apostles preached.

The God revealed to us in the Scriptures is *sovereign*. The first thing that the Bible tells us is: 'In the beginning, God created . . .' He is declared to be the sovereign Creator of all things, and this fact is made plain before any of his other attributes – justice, holiness, mercy, love – are revealed. By 'sovereign' is meant 'supreme', and God is sovereign because 'He worketh all things after the counsel of his own will',[4] not out of necessity, but

2. Acts 20:27   3. Rom. 1:1, 16, 17; Acts 14:3; Eph. 1:13
4. Eph. 1:11

freely, for his own glory. Creation was a sovereign act, because its cause was solely the good pleasure of God.[5] God's word is: 'My counsel shall stand, and I will do all my pleasure',[6] and to that perfect will, all things, and all men, are subject. 'I will work, and who shall hinder it?'[7]

In the words of the Westminster Confession (V, 1):

'God, the great Creator of all things, doth uphold, direct, dispose and govern all creatures, actions and things, from the greatest even to the least, by his most wise and holy providence. . . . and the free and immutable counsel of his own will, to the praise of the glory of his wisdom, power, justice, goodness and mercy.'

That the providence of God extends to all things necessarily entails that human sinful acts are subject to God's will; this is the teaching of Scripture, for Peter's words at Pentecost are: 'Him, being delivered by the determinate counsel and foreknowledge of God, ye have taken, and by wicked hands have crucified and slain.'[8] Here it is clearly shown that God's providence in no way lessens man's responsibility for his sin. So also, Pharaoh was raised up in order that God might show in him his power, and manifest his name;[9] and while God says: 'I will harden Pharaoh's heart, and multiply my signs and my wonders in the land of Egypt',[10] we also read: 'But when Pharaoh saw that there was respite, *he* hardened his heart'.[11] God is emphatically not the author of sin; according to his holiness, he hates it, and judges it right-eously. The almighty God revealed to us in Scripture is a

5. Rev. 4:11; Ps. 33:6-9; Rom. 11:36   6. Is. 46:10
7. Is. 43:13; cf Is. 14:27; 2 Chr. 20:6
8. Acts 2:23; cf. Acts 4:27–28   9. Ex. 9:16   10. Ex. 7:3
11. Ex. 8:15, cf. v. 32

God who 'doeth according to his will in the army of heaven, and among the inhabitants of the earth; and none can stay his hand, or say unto him, What doest thou?'.[12]

The final cause of all God's purposes is the manifestation of his own glory. In particular, our creation, redemption, sanctification and glorification were all purposed for the glory of God first and foremost,[13] and to the questions 'Why did God create the world?', 'Why did he permit the occurrence of sin?', 'Why was salvation provided for men, and not for angels?', 'Why among those who hear the Gospel do some receive, and some reject it?', there is only one answer we can give – because thus it seemed good in the eyes of God, for a more perfect revelation of his nature and perfections. That is not to say, of course, that God has no concern for men in his dealings with them; far from that! God is loving and beneficent to all men, as is clearly taught by Christ:[14] 'Love your enemies, and do them good, and lend, never despairing; and your reward shall be great, and ye shall be sons of the Most High: for he is kind toward the unthankful and evil. Be ye merciful, even as your Father is merciful.' And his saving grace is the expression of even deeper love. God's love for his people is no less great or incomprehensible because it glorifies him; neither are our feelings of joy and peace any less real and wonderful because they are the result of, and not the primary purpose of, our salvation. God's ultimate purpose in working all things after the counsel of his own will is not our wellbeing; yet we know that our highest good is the result of his providential care of his children.[15]

12. Dan. 4:35   13. Eph. 2:8–10; Is. 61:1–3; Jn. 15:8
14. Lk. 6:35–36; cf. Mt. 5:45   15. Rom. 8:28

We will pause here for a moment, and consider what has so far been said. To some, this doctrine of the sovereignty of God which we have just propounded may seem a little extreme; to others, perhaps, quite dreadful. To the carnal mind – to that old nature within us – the idea that man is utterly in the hands of God, to whom it belongs to direct the whole future of a man, seems abhorrent; such a thought will not be countenanced at any price, for surely man is free, is he not, to do exactly as he pleases? We will shortly return to this problem; suffice it to say that belief in the absolute sovereignty of God is required of all those who would seek to hold thoroughly Scriptural beliefs, for this great doctrine is imprinted on every verse of Holy Scripture from Genesis to Revelation. Although our reason, and our natural inclinations, might lead us to reject it, or to modify it, yet the truth is there, firmly embedded in God's Word. We are not bound to explain the doctrine; Martin Luther's dictum 'Because God says so, I will believe that it is so; I will follow the Word, and regard my own thoughts and ideas as vain' is ours as well. Nevertheless, we would venture to suggest four reasons, beyond the bare fact that the truth is in Scripture, for holding it:

Because the idea that God could be 'King of kings and Lord of lords',[16] the One 'in whose sight all things are open and manifest',[17] and yet be a God to whom all things were not subject, is inconceivable. If God's nature is unchanging,[18] and his act of creation was a sovereign act, it follows that he is still sovereign over what he has created, being not merely its Creator, but its Sustainer and Ruler.[19]

Because it is pointless to claim and hold fast to the

16. Rev. 19:16   17. Heb. 4:13   18. Mal. 3:6
19. Heb. 1:3; Acts 17:24–28

promises of God as given in his Word, if they are made by One who is in fact *not* sovereign, and therefore not sure of being able to keep them, being bound by the free-will man has been given, which God will never invade. No! The promises of our God are sure and steadfast and trustworthy; we claim them because their Author is our sovereign Lord himself.[20]

Because it reduces prayer to mere wishful thinking if God is powerless to answer our prayers; it is pointless to pray for the conversion of a soul, if God is not sovereign in redemption.

Because it is a truth that glorifies God, and God is pleased to honour and prosper the one who honours and fears him for what he is declared to be – sovereign.

We are convinced that a right understanding of this truth about God is the fountainhead from which a right understanding about every other doctrine follows, and, more important, from which a right relationship between the sinner and his Saviour stems. Speaking of much modern evangelicalism, Dr. J. I. Packer has well said that its message 'conspicuously fails to produce deep reverence, deep repentance, deep humility, a spirit of worship, a concern for the church. Why? We would suggest that the reason lies in its own character and content. It fails to make men God-centred in their thoughts, and God-fearing in their hearts, because this is not primarily what it is trying to do . . . It is too exclusively concerned to be "helpful" to man – to bring peace, comfort, happiness, satisfaction – and too little concerned to glorify God.' We are accustomed to hearing a rather glib 'All things work together for good . . .' whenever a disaster befalls. But at all times due attention to the glorious truth set before us

20. 2 Cor. 1:20; Ex. 12:25; Ps. 119:89–91

in Romans 8:28 would cause us to fall down on our knees in humble amazement and adoration before the great God who condescends to concern himself with every aspect of our lives. 'If then I be a father, where is mine honour?',[21] while his promises of blessing to those who honour him still stand firm.[22]

The God revealed to us in the Scriptures is, further, *holy*, *just*, and *righteous*. He is a God who *reveals his wrath against sin, and judges it*. The holiness of God is incomparable and is exhibited in the Law, and in the life and character of Jesus Christ.[23] God requires of men that they should be holy as he is holy,[24] and that they should obey the Law, failure to do which is precisely the sin of mankind.[25] The justice of God requires that all sin be punished,[26] the condemnation being borne, however, for those who are saved, by the Lord Jesus Christ,[27] while those who die in their sins are themselves condemned to eternal separation from God.[28]

Again, the God revealed to us in the Scriptures is *merciful* and *loving*.[29] If a man is saved, it is because of God's mercy in forgiving him his sins.[30] The God who is love, although he could justly condemn all mankind to death, yet has delivered from that condemnation a great multitude which no man can number, delivering them out of darkness, and from the power of Satan, bringing them into his marvellous light, the Kingdom of his Son.[31] This is the mercy and the love of God toward sinners, the very centre of the Gospel.

21. Mal. 1:6   22. 1 Sam. 2:30
23. 1 Sam. 2:2; Heb. 7:26   24. Gen. 17:1; Lev. 11:44
25. 1 Jn. 3:4   26. Gal. 3:10; Acts 17:31   27. Gal. 3:13
28. Jn. 3:36; Mt. 25:46; Jn. 5:29   29. Ex. 34:6; Jn. 3:16
30. Eph. 2:4; Tit. 3:5   31. 1 Pet. 2:8–9; Col. 1:13

Richard Sibbes, commenting on God's title 'the Father of mercies' in 2 Corinthians 1:3, writes:

'Every thing that comes from God to his children, it is a mercy. It is as it were dipt in mercy before it comes to us. It is a mercy, that is, there is a freedom in it, and a pity to his creature. For the creature is alway in some necessity and in some dependence. We are in a state of necessities in this life, in some misery or other, and that, as I said, is the object of mercy.

'Besides, we are dependent for the good we have. It is at God's mercy to continue or to take away any comfort that he gives us. Every thing is a mercy. And in every thing we take from God we ought to conceive a mercy in it, and to think this is a mercy from God. If we have health, it is a mercy; if we have strength, it is a mercy; if we have deliverance, it is a mercy. It comes in the respect and relation of a mercy, all that comes from God. He is not said to be the father of the thing; but the "Father of mercies". There is a mercy contained in the thing. They come from the pity and love of God, and that is the sweetest. Therefore, he is said to be the "Father of mercies." . . .

' "Father of mercies." In a corrupt estate the special mercy is forgiving mercy. If it were not for forgiving mercies, all other gifts and mercies were to little purpose. For it were but a reserving of us to eternal judgement, but a feeding the traitor to the day of execution, a giving him the liberty of the prison, which is nothing unless his treason be pardoned. So the forgiving mercy leads to all the rest. Now these forgiving mercies, they are unlimited mercies, there is no bounds of them. For he being the Father of Christ, who is an infinite person, and having received an infinite satisfaction from an infinite person, he may well be infinitely merciful; and himself is an infinite

God. His mercies are like himself. The satisfaction whereby he may be merciful is infinite. Hereupon it is that he may pardon, and will pardon all sin without limitation, if they be never so great, never so many.'

It may be objected that this discussion of God's character is unbalanced. So it is – we have dwelt at some length upon the sovereignty of God, and said little about his holiness and love. This is intentional – our purpose is not to provide a complete theology of salvation, but rather to call to remembrance certain Biblical truths which, we feel, are frequently forgotten, ignored or misunderstood in these days.

QUESTIONS AND OBJECTIONS CONSIDERED

Many things occur which are against God's will

The argument is this: All sinful acts, of men and demons, occur against God's will, for Scripture makes it plain that God is not the author of sin, nor does he connive at it, for he is holy; on the contrary, he hates and abhors sin. But if things occur which are against God's will, he cannot exercise *de facto* sovereignty over these things. Therefore his sovereignty is not absolute, but limited in its exercise. (No-one denies, of course, that God has *de jure* sovereignty over all things; we are discussing whether he exercises it.)

The fallacy of this argument lies in the ambiguity of the term 'God's will'. There is a distinction which must be made between God's decretive will and his preceptive will; that is, between his will which determines what he will actually do or permit, as Governor of the world, which is a secret will; and his will declared to his rational and responsible creatures as to what they ought to do. Now, these are not always the same; *not* because God only pretends to want man to do good, having secretly planned that he should do evil, but because he sees and decides, in his wisdom and goodness, that it will be better – more to his glory – to permit and overrule sin for the accomplishment of his own purposes. So that actual sin, while always against God's precepts, is never against his will in the sense of his decrees as to what shall come to pass; and he is sovereign over all.

These things are mysteries indeed, but are to be accepted on the authority of God's Word. In the case previously discussed of the crucifixion, it is clear from Matthew 26:24 that God hated Judas' sin, and yet that Judas' action was foreordained by him. Thus it was that the Lord Jesus could say that he laid down his life of his own accord, no-one taking it from him – that is, not against his will – even though man's sinful acts were a necessary means to that end.[32]

God is made responsible for sin

It is objected that, if God sovereignly overrules and ordains all things, then he becomes responsible for all events, and is thus responsible for, and in a real sense the author of, sin. This is contrary to Scripture, so God cannot be absolutely sovereign.

We agree that God is not the author of sin. Therefore his sovereignty must be understood consistently with this fact, and we may not say that he is the immediate or effective cause of any sinful action. When we say that God ordains a sinful action, this means that he is the cause of it only in a restricted sense, in that he decides

32. Jn. 10:18

to allow a responsible (i.e. accountable) agent thus to act.

If it is said that God is responsible for sin even so, because he foresees the sin as a consequence of his direct action of foreordination, we reply that this argument is contrary to all common sense and human analogy. 'A righteous judge, in passing sentence on a criminal, may be sure that he will cause wicked and bitter feelings in the criminal's mind, or in the hearts of his friends, and yet the judge be guiltless. A father, in excluding a reprobate son from his family, may see that the inevitable consequence of such exclusion will be his greater wickedness, and yet the father may do right' (C. Hodge).

It must, of course, be understood that God's foreordination is *not* compulsion (see below, p. 31). If it were, then God would be responsible for all the consequences.

If God is absolutely sovereign, why do we need to pray?

The fact of God's absolute sovereignty has a great bearing on the subject of prayer. Much current teaching on prayer would have us believe that God will not and cannot bring to pass his eternal purposes unless we pray. As one modern author puts it: 'The possibilities and necessity of prayer, its power and results, are manifested in arresting and changing the purposes of God and in relieving the stroke of his power.' Apparently, we are to believe that God's policy is shaped by the prayers of men. Sinful and corrupt human beings are able to change the sovereign purposes and plans of an almighty and holy God! Not only is this kind of teaching an affront to the honour and glory of our mighty Lord and Creator, it also directly contravenes the words of Holy Scripture – 'My counsel shall stand, and I will accomplish all my purpose.'[33] The God we worship is not someone who is constantly shaping his purposes and changing his plans as a result of the wishes of men, because with him 'there is no variation or shadow due to change.'[34] 'I the LORD change not.'[35] God's designs and purposes are unchangeable and eternal.

But the inevitable question arises. If God is absolutely sovereign over human affairs, why do we need to pray at all? If it is true that 'of him, and through him, and unto him, are all things',[36] then surely there would appear to be no point in prayer. Yet, God tells us to pray – 'Pray without ceasing',[37] and again, 'Men ought always to pray'.[38] We read in James 5:15 that 'the prayer of faith shall save him that is sick', and in the following verse that 'the supplication of a righteous man availeth much in its working'. The Lord Jesus Christ himself was supremely a Man of prayer. How then do we reconcile God's sovereignty with the need for Christian prayer?

We have seen that God in his infinite purposes has decreed that certain events shall come to pass, but he has also decreed that these events shall come to pass through appointed means. God has elected certain people to be saved, but he has also decreed that they shall be saved through the preaching of the Gospel. In the very same epistle to the Romans, in which Paul expounds the doctrine of God's absolute sovereignty in the salvation of men, he also stresses the vital need and responsibility for men to preach the Gospel. 'How then shall they call on him in whom they have not believed? and how shall

33. Is. 46:10   34. Jas. 1:17   35. Mal. 3:6
36. Rom. 11:36   37. 1 Thess. 5:17   38. Lk. 18:1

they believe in him of whom they have not heard? and how shall they hear without a preacher?'[39] The preaching of the Gospel is the appointed means for the working out of the eternal purposes of God. Prayer is another means. God has decreed the means as well as the end, and among the means is prayer. And so, instead of prayers being in vain, they are among the means through which God fulfils his decrees. The design of prayer is not to change God's will, but to accomplish it. The Lord Jesus knew that after his death and resurrection he would be exalted by the Father. Yet we find him asking for this very thing – 'Now, O Father, glorify thou me with thine own self with the glory which I had with thee before the world was.'[40] The spirit in which we pray should be 'Not my will, but thine, be done.'[41]

We can now understand more fully the reason for so-called 'unanswered' prayers. God's answer and his will may often be the very opposite of what would be most acceptable to the flesh. 'If we ask anything *according to his will*, he heareth us.'[42] James says – 'You ask and do not receive, because you ask wrongly, to spend it on your passions.'[43] As we grow in grace and in the fuller knowledge of God, then his desires will become our desires, and our prayers will be in accordance with his will. 'If ye abide in me, and my words abide in you, ask whatever ye will, and it shall be done unto you.'[44]

'Prayer is not the requesting of God to alter his purpose or for him to form a new one. Prayer is the taking of an attitude of dependency upon God, the spreading of our need before him, and the asking for those things which are in accordance with his will; therefore, there is noth-

39. Rom. 10:14   40. Jn. 17:5   41. Lk. 22:42
42. 1 Jn. 5:14   43. Jas. 4:3   44. Jn. 15:7

ing whatever inconsistent between Divine sovereignty and Christian prayer' (A. W. Pink).

A recognition of God's sovereignty should make us more, not less zealous, in prayer. It is because God has promised certain things, that we can ask for them with the full assurance of faith. A true recognition of this doctrine will also result in a greater desire to worship and praise our sovereign Lord. Real prayer is an act of worship – an acknowledgement of his goodness, power, and grace, and a submission to his will. Real prayer is coming into the presence of God and realizing our total unworthiness.

Prayer is designed by God for our humbling and for his glory. It is a means of spiritual blessing and growth in grace. To regard the purpose of prayer as simply our seeking from God the things of which we are in need, is to consider prayer only from the human side. Prayer also needs to be viewed from the Divine side. 'Lord, teach us to pray.'

God's foreordination implies a denial of human responsibility

Many of the problems arising in this whole subject spring from wrong or ambiguous definitions and ideas of determinism, responsibility, and freedom. We must define terms carefully in order to make the distinctions which are necessary to a right understanding of these concepts. The doctrine of God's sovereign foreordination may be called determinism if by this is meant that whatever God foreordains must necessarily come to pass. This is true. But it is not to be equated with fatalism, which makes fate control events in a way independent of secondary agents or causes, which amounts to compulsion. We repeat that foreordination is not compulsion; and man is therefore rightly called a free agent. By a free agent we mean one who is free (not subject to external compulsion) to do whatever he wishes. With obvious limitations, man is free in this sense. Clearly, therefore, God's foreordination is well and wisely adapted to the nature of man as a responsible, free agent, and encompasses man's will as well as his actions. To this there is considerable Scriptural testimony.[45]

It may be said, however, that the objection is deeper than this. Granted that the absence of compulsion gives man freedom in one sense of the word; nevertheless, if foreordination entails necessity, then man is not free to act except as God has foreordained. Therefore man cannot be held responsible for his actions.

We agree that man is not free in such an absolute sense as to be independent of God, but deny the conclusion that he is not responsible. Indeed, if it is said that necessity implies no responsibility, God's foreordination is not the only doctrine that must be rejected: his foreknowledge of events equally makes them necessary. Yet Divine foreknowledge is an attribute to deny which not only blasphemes the perfection of God, but overthrows Scriptural testimony both direct and indirect. If God cannot foreknow events which depend on responsible, secondary agents, then he cannot cause men to prophesy such events: yet the Bible is full of such prophecies.

There is, then, no contradiction between necessity and man's responsibility (for Scripture demands that we hold to both); nor between God's sovereign foreordination and man's responsibility.

45. Lam. 3:37; Prov. 16:1; 21:1; Jer. 10:23; Phil. 2:13

Man

The truth about the nature of man is an outstanding example of the necessity to adhere faithfully to the over-all teaching of Scripture, as it is here that a wrong understanding leads necessarily and logically to false or inadequate views about regeneration, the atonement, sanctification, and the whole plan of salvation. How easily this occurs, and how it is occurring around us, will be shown in subsequent pages. For the moment, we shall concern ourselves with what the Bible teaches about this all-important subject. Man needs to see his situation in correct perspective. He is incapable of reaching a correct understanding of that situation intuitively. He needs to view it, so to speak, from the outside. As a fallen creature, he can only obtain a complete and correct view of himself by revelation; in other words, by reference to what God has spoken of him.

The teaching of Scripture is clear and unequivocal. Man is *totally depraved*; that is to say, the fall of Adam, in which all men participate,[46] extends to *all* man's faculties:[47] his *heart* (which in Scripture denotes the very centre of man's being — the seat of his affections and personality),[48] his *mind*,[49] his *will*,[50] his *conscience*,[51] and every other part of him. Sin is described as being a *state* of enmity against God, and of transgression of his commandments,[52] and, forasmuch as fallen men have no power of themselves to think, speak or will anything that may please God, until they be regenerate and renewed by the Spirit of the Lord, all works done before justification

46. 1 Cor. 15:21–22; Rom. 5:12–21   47. Is. 1:5–6
48. Mt. 15:19; Jer. 17:9   49. Eph. 4:17–18; Rom. 1:28
50. Jn. 5:40   51. Tit. 1:15
52. Dan. 9:9–11; Rom. 1:29–32

have the nature of sin, as the Anglican Prayer-Book Article XIII says. 'They that are in the flesh cannot please God.'[53] There is therefore *not a single thing that a man can do* that will please God, if he has not been born again. Every man, woman and child born into this world, with the exception of our Lord, is a slave to sin,[54] is dead in sin,[55] sins in all things,[56] and cannot cease from sin until God in his mercy delivers him or her from it.

The sinfulness of man does not consist solely of the voluntary sins which he commits; for these are the fruits of his corrupt nature.[57] Empirically, we observe daily that sin abounds; but the Scriptures reveal to us that the situation is infinitely more desperate than we could ever have realized. Man's sin is not only what he does – which we can see – but what he *is*, which we cannot see as God sees it.

At this point, an objection may be made by some: If man is totally depraved, and cannot but sin, while, as we asserted above, God's providence rules the actions of men, does it not follow that man's sin is something that man cannot be held responsible for? Is not God, then, the author of sin?

These are important questions, and we will not attempt to avoid them, but to tackle them later. But a few remarks here will be appropriate.

It is noteworthy that Adam's reply to God, when asked if he had disobeyed God's commandment not to eat of the fruit of the tree of the knowledge of good and evil, was, in effect, to put the blame upon God. 'The woman,

---

53. Rom. 8:8   54. Ps. 51:5; Rom. 3:9–20; Jn. 8:34
55. Gen. 2:17; Eph. 2:1   56. Ezek. 21:24
57. Jas. 1:14; Eph. 2:2–3; Mt. 15:19

whom thou gavest to be with me, she gave me of the tree, and I did eat.'[58] The unregenerate man, like Adam, attempts to cover his transgressions by objecting: 'Why doth he still find fault? . . . Why didst thou make me thus?' The answer of Scripture to such talk is: 'O man, who art thou that repliest against God?' 'Woe unto him that striveth with his Maker!'[59] We are not bound to explain these things, but to hold both to the impossibility of not sinning, apart from the grace of God, and to the fact that God holds man utterly responsible for his sin, and will condemn him, unless he flees to him for mercy.

The problems centre around what for centuries has been a theological and philosophical minefield – 'free-will'. A common argument runs as follows:

God holds man responsible for his sin.

Man cannot be held responsible for something he cannot refrain from doing.

therefore: Man's will must be free to choose between sinning, and not sinning; and hence, to choose between 'accepting' Christ, or rejecting him.

We would assert that this conclusion is false, and highly dangerous, because of the falsity of the second premise, namely, that man can only be held responsible for what he has the *ability* to perform. We hold that this is false for two reasons:

First – Because Scripture denies it. We have already seen that man's will, like every other part of him, is depraved, and *in bondage* to sin. Anything that is in bondage evidently cannot be free. Man's will, therefore, being part of a dead nature, is not free towards God in any sense,

58. Gen. 3:12   59. Rom. 9:19–20; Is. 45:9

but is 'free' only to sin. Paul says absolutely: 'They that are in the flesh *cannot* please God'; Job says: 'Who can bring a clean thing out of an unclean? not one.'[60] Neither is man free to turn to Christ for mercy – he cannot, of his own volition. The one thing that, above all others, surely pleases God, that thing over which the angels of heaven rejoice, is the sight of a sinner turning to God, and repenting. Yet, men in the flesh cannot do this; it is impossible: God's Word says so. Notwithstanding, God commands and requires all men everywhere to repent of their sins,[61] and will judge them if they do not do so. God, who is righteous, will only judge a man for something for which he is responsible.

Second – Because 'free-will' and responsibility are different things. If, by 'freedom of the will', what is meant is 'freedom of action', i.e. that when I do something, I do it freely, without compulsion or constraint; then, it is agreed, man is a free agent, and is responsible, precisely because he is not forced to act *against* his volitions. 'Freedom', in this sense, therefore means nothing more than the harmony that exists, normally, between a man's volitions and his actions. If I am at gunpoint to rob a bank, then I am not responsible for my action, since I acted under compulsion, *against* my (law-abiding) volitions *not* to do so. Clearly, when a man sins, his *will* and his actions are united in sinning, and so man is to be held responsible for his sin. His volition and his action are both results of the corrupt nature which is his. But then, 'free-will' is a misnomer, and a misleading term to express the liberty of spontaneity which man does possess.

The notion that man is responsible only for what he has the ability to perform is utterly false. The fact that

60. Job 14:4   61. Acts 17:30

sinful actions spring inevitably from a sinful nature is no excuse; it rather aggravates the guilt. For man's sinful nature is no part of God's original creation, and man's duty (by which responsibility is to be judged) is determined by God's moral law, which unfallen man could keep. The fall and its consequences do not lessen our responsibility; they increase it. Our sin in Adam[62] has rendered us unable to do good, yet the sinner, each one of us, is accountable to God in every respect, thought, word and deed. God commands us to render complete obedience and satisfaction to the moral law of the ten commandments. That we cannot do so is patently obvious. Nevertheless, it is required.

Man, then, in all his faculties, is as chained and imprisoned in the darkness of his sins, in captivity to Satan, as Peter was bound by Herod on the eve of his intended execution;[63] as dead as Lazarus in the tomb;[64] as blind as the man Jesus healed.[65] We must be on our guard against the theory that man's will is free, and not bound, or dead, or corrupted – and hence, that man *can* please God, if he wills to do so – for Scripture is against such a theory.

Man, then, is responsible for his sin, and he is under the condemnation of God. Even if man offended in only one part of the Law, he would be under sentence of death, for 'Cursed is everyone that continueth not in all things that are written in the book of the law, to do them.'[66] That condemnation which, but for the mercy of God, would be the just deserts of each one of us is declared in Scripture to entail a place of torment, of weeping and gnashing of teeth, of everlasting fire, of eternal

62. Rom. 5:12–21   63. Acts 12   64. Jn. 11
65. Jn. 9   66. Gal. 3:10

separation from God.[67] These are truths about which we hear little, yet the Word of God plainly declares them. Scripture knows nothing of universal salvation, or of the annihilation of the wicked, or of purgatory, of a second chance, and so on. The truth set before us is one of condemnation to eternal punishment. The plight of man, therefore, is truly dreadful. Unless he repents of his sin, and believes on the Lord Jesus Christ, he is heading straight for hell. God commands, exhorts, beseeches him to repent and believe, in order that his soul might be saved; yet man cannot and will not do so. He is 'fast bound in sin and nature's night', unable to lift a finger towards the attainment of his salvation. Yet only as he sees himself shut in between the condemning finger of the Law, which shows him to be a miserable sinner, and the command of God to flee from his sin and lay hold of Christ, which he cannot obey,[68] does he see his true condition, and consequently, the direction from which deliverance must come.

QUESTIONS AND OBJECTIONS CONSIDERED

Experience shows that man can do and will do that which is good

The doctrine of total depravity is not that every man is as bad as he could possibly be; but that man's nature is corrupted and disabled in every part and aspect – his mind and will as well as his body, affections, etc. So we do not deny that the natural man is capable of doing and willing things which are in themselves good. This is an effect of God's 'common grace' – that is, the work of the

67. Rev. 14: 10–11; Mt. 24:51; 25:41; 3:12; Rev. 21:8
68. Rom. 2:8–12; Jn. 6:44

Holy Spirit in restraining men from sin and in leading them to do good, which extends to all men. Such grace is necessary to prevent the world from sinking into a condition as evil as hell itself; yet it is not the same as saving grace, and the good which results is despite the sinners' corrupt nature.

These good deeds are not acceptable to God, because they are without the only motive with which God is pleased – love to God and humble faith in Christ.[69] When the Pharisaical Jews kept every outward commandment of the Law, they were doing that with which God is indeed pleased, in itself – but he was not pleased with them, because every act was marred by the sinful and unsuspected enmity of their hearts.[70] Their best deeds were as filthy rags in the sight of our Holy God.[71] Prayer is pleasing and honouring to God; yet he will not hear the prayer of the wicked.[72] The unsaved man may do good works in order to obtain reputation; or to justify himself before God or man; or to quieten his conscience and silence the pangs of conviction of sin; or from the working of the common grace of God in him: he will *never* do good works to glorify God, from a grateful, penitent heart, for it is against his corrupt nature. Can an evil tree bring forth good fruit?[73]

The commands of Scripture imply ability

This inference hardly deserves refutation, but simply denial. The sphere of moral ability is quite different from that of natural ability. The commands of Scripture imply moral *responsibility* or *duty*; and in no way does 'I ought' imply 'I can'.

69. Heb. 11:6   70. Jer. 17:9   71. Is. 64:6
72. Prov. 28:9   73. Lk. 6:43–45

If man's inability to obey the commands of the Law were natural or physical, he would indeed lack responsibility, and there would be no point in commanding him to do that of which he is absolutely incapable. But 'as the inability of the sinner to repent and believe, to love God and to lead a holy life, does not arise from the limitation of his nature as a creature (as is the case with idiots or brutes); nor from the want of the requisite faculties or capacity, but simply from the corruption of our nature, it follows that it does not exonerate him from the obligation to be and to do all that God requires' (C. Hodge). A sinful nature imposes a moral inability as inflexible as prison bars, yet the sinner is responsible to do that which his own fallen nature renders impossible. If it were not so, a man would become less and less responsible as he became more and more sinful – an absurd conclusion which would make the punishment of Satan quite unjust.

It is worth adding that there *is* a point in commanding sinners to obey, even though they cannot do so. For through the Law comes discovery of sin in all its sinfulness.[74] The sinner who realizes his condition, his guilt under the Law, may be driven by the Holy Spirit to Christ for refuge. It is just as when Christ called 'Lazarus, come forth!': Lazarus was dead; he could not obey; yet in that instant he was quickened by the power of God, and came forth.[75]

A closely related argument is that responsibility for sin implies that one could have avoided sinning. The answer is again very simple: responsibility for sin implies that one *ought* not to have sinned. When the unregenerate man sins, he does so freely, as a free agent, and in accordance with his own wishes; and it is this which

74. Rom. 7:13   75. Jn. 11:43–44

makes him responsible. It is true that his action is doubly necessary – necessary as all events are, because foreordained of God; and necessary because of the corruption of his enslaved nature – but *moral* necessity in no way limits responsibility.

2

THE WAY OF SALVATION

We turn now to show how the redemption, accomplished at the cross of Golgotha, is *applied* to the individual; in other words, how, according to Scripture, man is saved.

A revealing example of the character of men under the dominion of Satan and in their natural state is provided by the madman of Gadara, who, 'when he saw Jesus, cried out, and fell down before him, and with a loud voice said, What have I to do with thee, Jesus, thou Son of the Most High God?', and by the local inhabitants who, when Jesus had performed the miracle, begged him to depart from them.[1] Because the mind of the flesh is enmity against God,[2] spiritual things are hateful to him – he cannot will to be saved, because his will is 'ruled over by the iron lusts of his own heart'. Never was this more forcefully expressed than by the Lord Jesus himself: 'Ye will not come to me, that ye might have life',[3] an eloquent expression of the fallen state of man. The condemnation is that, because of his plunge into sin, man is *un*-willing to lay hold of eternal life. The Gospel says: 'Whosoever will, let him take of the water of life freely',[4] while sinful man testifies to a universal 'whosoever will not'. It is evident, then, that, far from the Lord Jesus Christ waiting patiently and impotently at the door of our life for us to make up our minds to let him in, if left to our 'free-will' we would be for ever lost, and no one could be saved. Yet God, in his mercy, *delivers, saves*

1. Lk. 8:28, 37   2. Rom. 8:7   3. Jn. 5:40; cf. Mt. 23:37
4. Rev. 22:17

sinners from that death, by drawing them to himself. This is the work of the Holy Spirit, the Lord and Giver of life, a work of *irresistible grace*, an *effectual call*, by which a man embraces the salvation Christ won for him, by which he is truly born again of the Spirit of God. 'No man can come to me' (because of his hardness of heart, and sinful unwillingness) 'except the Father draw him'.[5]

The Gospel command to repent and believe in Jesus Christ is addressed to all men, without exception. The gracious invitations of the Lord Jesus Christ are without any restriction: 'Come unto me, all ye that labour and are heavy laden . . .'[6] Manifestly, not all men do come to Jesus Christ, as he himself said,[7] owing to their unwillingness; yet he testifies that in salvation, as in all other things, God is sovereign: 'All that the Father giveth me shall come to me, and him that cometh to me I will in no wise cast out'.[8] Those who come to Christ do so because they have been *drawn* by the Holy Spirit, given new life by him. 'The letter' (i.e. the Law) 'killeth, but the Spirit giveth life.'[9] Regeneration, the new birth, must, then, be wholly the work of the Holy Spirit, in which there is no room for human co-operation. A man can no more assist, or will, his regeneration than he can his natural birth, or than a dead man, such as Lazarus, can assist in his resurrection. Man's natural inclination is to resist the Holy Spirit's work,[10] and if the words 'new birth', and the entire metaphor, have any meaning at all, they signify that, although a man must be born again, – and unless he is born of water and of the Spirit he cannot see the Kingdom of God – yet it is totally outside his power to effect, to will or to desire the new birth, for what man has

5. Jn. 6:44   6. Mt. 11:28; cf. Jn. 7:37   7. Jn. 5:40
8. Jn. 6:37   9. 2 Cor. 3:6   10. Acts 7:51

ever effected, willed or desired his natural birth? Man, a
helpless and vile sinner, is utterly at the mercy of the
Holy Spirit, who, like the wind, 'bloweth where it listeth,
and thou hearest the sound thereof, but canst not tell
whence it cometh, and whither it goeth'.[11] This is the
truth Jesus sought to impress on Nicodemus, to rid him of
the supposition that he could be saved anywhere, any
time, whenever he felt the need. We repeat that man's
will is *not* free with respect to the things of God, or to
his salvation: his will is in bondage to sin, for 'the natural
man receiveth not the things of the Spirit of God . . .'[12]
Salvation is '*not of him that willeth*, nor of him that
runneth, but of God that hath mercy'.[13] '*Of his own will
begat he us* with the word of truth';[14] who were born 'not
of blood, nor of the will of the flesh, nor of the will of
man, but of God'.[15]

We are now in a position to see the dangers into which
a wrong or inadequate view of the sin and corruption of
man can lead us. No longer would it then be 'not by
works of righteousness which we have done, but according to his mercy'[16] that he saved us, but it would be
salvation conditional upon the free-will of man – of man
allowing God to save him at his – a sinner's – pleasure. 'I
will put my Spirit in you, and ye shall live'[17] is the Biblical Gospel of the grace of God which saves sinners just as
as they are – guilty, vile, helpless, deserving only of
wrath and damnation. It is not the Biblical Gospel that
makes salvation dependent upon what I do; this is salvation by works, for if my salvation depends on my choosing

11. Jn. 3:1–15   12. 1 Cor. 2:14   13. Rom. 9:16
14. Jas. 1:18   15. Jn. 1:13   16. Tit. 3:5
17. Ezek. 37:14

Christ, while he waits for my decision, then, by comparison with my neighbour who is not saved, I must have done something to achieve my salvation which he has not done; in which case I have cause for boasting, and my salvation is the direct result of *my* decision. Such a theory is, unfortunately, very common, but this is not the New Testament Gospel; this Gospel is gloriously *free*; it is a Gospel which proclaims salvation all of GRACE, a Gospel which we can take to all men, however black their sins.[18] As long as salvation depends on man's will, it is a gospel of works, the gospel which the Galatians were in danger of adopting, and which Paul so abhorred.[19] The supposed gospel of free-will seeks to bring it within the power of all men to be saved; the Biblical Gospel of free-grace proclaims the impotence of all human activity, so that sinners cast themselves wholly upon the mercies of God for forgiveness.

Although the purpose of God in saving sinners can never be frustrated,[20] and those whom God effectually calls infallibly come to him,[21] the term 'irresistible grace' is a slightly misleading way of referring to the work of divine grace in the human heart; for this work of the Holy Spirit is precisely to remove the sinful will to resist him, so that when a man is saved, he comes to Christ willingly, and with joy receives his salvation.[22]

But, it may be objected, what has all this to do with the simple command of the Gospel to repent and believe? The promise of eternal life is made to all who *believe*,[23] so surely repentance and faith are necessary for eternal life, and so must precede the new birth?

18. Eph. 2:8; 1 Tim. 1:15   19. Gal. 1:8–9
20. Is. 43:13   21. Jn. 6: 37; Rom. 8:29–30
22. Phil. 2:13; Deut. 30:6   23. Jn. 3:16

That repentance and faith are necessary for salvation is clear from Scripture,[24] and the Gospel which the apostles preached, and which we must preach, was a universal call to repent and believe. But we deny that man has any more natural ability to obey these commands to respond to the call of the Gospel, than he has to obey the Law. Man is far too corrupt to repent of his sins and turn to Christ, just as he is too corrupt to obey the Law as God requires him. Scripture teaches that, while all who *do* repent and believe on the Lord Jesus Christ *shall* be saved, repentance and faith are gifts of God, and they *follow*, and do not precede, the new birth. But, as soon as the soul is born again of the Spirit of God, as soon as it sees his light and his beauty, repentance (turning from his former sins) and faith in the Lord Jesus Christ as a perfect Saviour well up in that soul as natural expressions of the new creation. Repentance is a sure sign of regeneration – for the loathing of and abandoning of sin can only come from the One who is without sin, who is light. It is impossible that man, who is in darkness, could ever of himself repent of his sins. 'Can an evil tree bring forth good fruit?' No – as soon as the heart of stone has been removed, and the heart of flesh implanted, repentance and faith follow, for the man has been made a partaker of the divine nature. *God* grants repentance and faith[25] – that faith by which a man is justified.[26] The fact that this saving faith is the gift of God, and the fruit of regeneration, enables Paul to say: 'Where then is the glorying? It is excluded.'[27] 'By grace are ye saved through faith; and that not of yourselves: it is the gift of God: not of works,

24. Acts 2:38; 16:31 *et al.*
25. Acts 11:18; cf. 2 Tim. 2:25; Phil. 1:29; cf. Acts 13:48
26. Rom. 3:26   27. Rom. 3:27

lest any man should boast.'[28] Man certainly would have cause to boast if repentance and faith were conditions, works, he had to perform in order to be born again. But the Gospel forbids it! God saves sinners who are on the road to perdition, and unable to do anything about it; and this of his mercy and grace!

It is important to understand clearly the *nature* of true saving faith. According to the Gospel, it is the means by which the sinner appropriates for himself the righteousness of Christ and thereby is declared to be 'justified' before God. Faith is the holding out to God of empty hands, in order to receive the white robes of salvation with which God has promised to clothe all who believe in his Son. But it is God himself who is the justifier of the ungodly; it is God who remembers no more the sins of the unrighteous; it is God who reckons the sinner as righteous on account of Christ's righteous life and obedience unto death. In short, faith is nothing more than the means by which the sinner apprehends and receives the blessings that flow to him because of the eternal love of the triune God. With the exercise of faith the scales fall from our eyes and we claim the Saviour of the world to be our own.

We have seen that saving faith comes to us through the working of the Holy Spirit. Even while we ascribe our faith entirely to him, however, we must not fall into the error of thinking that our justification is a *reward* for our having exercised faith in him. Romans chapter 4 makes it clear that, if the latter were the case, then faith exercised in Christ would itself become a work, *meriting* acceptance with God; and the distinction between works

28. Eph. 2:8–9

that merit, and faith that receives, which Paul is so anxious to draw, would be confused. The crucial distinction must be drawn between the work of Christ *for* us, in obtaining our salvation, and the work of the Spirit *in* us revealing that salvation to us, and enabling us to receive it. 'Faith justifies us, no, *not even as a gift of the Holy Ghost*, but solely on account of its reference to Christ' (Luther). A few words of Brentius, writing to Melanchthon, underlines the cardinal importance of this distinction:

'Justification comes to us neither *on account* of our love nor our faith, but solely on account of Christ; and yet it comes *through* (by means of) faith. Faith does not justify as a work of goodness, but simply as a receiver of promised mercy. . . . We do not *merit*, we only *obtain* justification. . . . Faith is but the organ, the instrument, the medium; Christ alone is the satisfaction and the merit.'

Justification by faith is the heart of the Gospel. This is what is contained in the promise, 'Whosoever believeth in him shall not perish, but have everlasting life.' If we fail to grasp the fact that the righteousness which justifies us is *imputed* and not infused or inherent, we shall find that, in substance, what we preach is a gospel of works, not a Gospel of grace.

A problem still remains: why are all sinners commanded to come to Christ, to repent of their sins, when they are not able to do so? This is the same problem that we met before, when considering and refuting the argument that responsibility implies ability. It is true that a man cannot come to Christ, except he be drawn by the Father; it is evident that not all men are saved, and hence, that not all men are drawn; it is also true that the sin of rejection of Christ is a sin for which man will be judged, a sin for which, then, he is responsible.[29] So then, the Gospel command is being addressed to sinners who are unable to help themselves. Precisely! These are truths which we are unable to reconcile – yet God requires us to hold firmly to both, and to preach both man's duty to believe the Gospel, and his sinful inability to do so; to deliver the command to sinners to believe on the Lord Jesus Christ for their salvation, and to proclaim that only grace can enable this. 'It is an axiom of theology that, if a man is saved, God must get all the glory for it; if he is condemned, God must not be blamed for it.' Sheer human inability to attain to a fulness of understanding makes these twin truths difficult to reconcile, but since both are indeed truths most evidently in agreement with the Word, they need no reconciliation from us.

This, then, is the Biblical scheme of things:

1. Christ is willing to save all who come to him for mercy; he commands all men to repent and believe.
2. Man is unwilling to come; he cannot repent and believe.
3. Man must be made willing to come; he must be made able to repent and believe.

Exhortation: Cast yourselves on the mercy of God, who alone can renew the heart and forgive sins; 'believe on the Lord Jesus'.[30]

QUESTIONS AND OBJECTIONS CONSIDERED

Scripture speaks of resisting the Holy Spirit, showing that it is possible to do so: Acts 7:51 'Ye do always resist the

29. Jn. 3:18, 19, 36; 16:8–9   30. Acts 16:31

Holy Ghost'; Eph. 4:30 'Grieve not the Holy Spirit of God'

We do not assert that *all* the operations of the Holy Spirit are irresistible. On the contrary, it is the very nature of unregenerate man *always* to resist the Holy Spirit, as Stephen says. The Spirit sent prophets: men rejected them and killed them. He applies convictions of sin to the heart: men stifle them. He causes Christ to be displayed in the Gospel: men will not hear.

Yet in all this the will of God is not overthrown, and in every case he accomplishes exactly what he intended. 'For who hath resisted his will?'[31] Conviction of sin in it-self has a tendency to conversion; so that he who stifles conviction resists the Holy Spirit. But in those whom he effectually calls out of darkness into light, he not only overcomes the resistance, he changes it into willing compliance.

Here is perhaps where the term 'irresistible grace' is misleading. For it is not that the sinner would like to resist, but cannot, because grace is too strong for him; no, that would be compulsion – conversion against one's will. Rather, when one is born again, the *whole* nature is changed, including the will, so that all resistance to the work of God vanishes, and the newly-regenerate man gladly accepts and runs to Christ by faith.

We return to the question, 'For who maketh thee to differ from another? and what hast thou that thou didst not receive?'[32] Is it that we ourselves make ourselves to differ, by our free-will response to the Spirit's pleading? Or is the whole glory of our salvation to belong to God alone? We were dead in trespasses and sins[33] – God alone can raise the dead to life; and we do not resist his resur-

31. Rom. 9:19   32. 1 Cor. 4:7   33. Eph. 2:1

rection power, for if we could, we *would*, and not one of us would be saved.

This eliminates free-will

For once we agree with the objection! Yes, the idol free-will, which pretends to direct the eternal destiny of mankind, is overthrown – and with it all grounds for human pride and boasting are cast down. Let us accept the simple, humbling testimony of the Scriptures that the mercy of God is 'not of him that willeth';[34] that God's children are born 'not of the will of man, but of God'.[35] The doctrines of irresistible grace and of God's unconditional election destroy free-will; just as David's stone, rightly aimed, eliminated Goliath, destroying once and for all the enemy of the people of God. 'Free-will' is not a friend, but an enemy; for the will of man, being corrupt, leads to his condemnation; man's true friend is the free-grace of God, which comes to his rescue, delivering him from the relentless tyranny of his own nature, from which he would otherwise be powerless to escape.

34. Rom. 9:16   35. Jn. 1:13

3

SALVATION PLANNED

As we have endeavoured to show, Scripture proclaims the sovereignty of the Lord. 'The Son quickeneth whom he will';[1] 'It is the Spirit that quickeneth; the flesh profiteth nothing'.[2] So, then, as men are unable, by reason of their sin, to come to Christ; as it is the Holy Spirit who effects the new birth in the heart of a man; as the purpose of God in saving sinners is always accomplished; and as all men are not saved; it is God, and not man, who decides who shall be saved: 'and he said, For this cause have I said unto you, that no man can come unto me, except it be given unto him of the Father.'[3] It was thus the will of God that some should be saved, while others he saw fit, 'according to the unsearchable counsel of his own will . . . for the glory of his sovereign power over his creatures, to pass by'. This is the Biblical truth of *unconditional election*. This follows naturally from what has so far been said about the total depravity of man, and the sovereignty of God. We, who are saved, are 'debtors to mercy alone', and the God who has saved us is the One who 'hath mercy on whom he will, and whom he will he hardeneth'.[4]

This is a hard truth – but then it is always hard to accept the humbling fact that God, and not man, ordains what shall be. Upon the words of the Lord Jesus Christ, that 'no man can come unto me, except it be given unto him of the Father', we read that 'many of his disciples

1. Jn. 5:21   2. Jn. 6:63   3. Jn. 6:37,64–65
4. Rom. 9:15–18

went back and walked no more with him'.[5] These sad
words testify to the fact that the carnal mind constantly
desires to assert itself against God in denying his sovereignty. As Spurgeon said, 'Many men cavil at election;
the very word with some is a great bugbear; they no
sooner hear it than they turn upon their heel for anger.
. . . But not all the sophisms of the learned, not all the
legerdemain of the cunning, will ever be able to sweep
the doctrine of election out of Holy Scripture.' And this is
the reason that we hold this or any other belief – because
it is Scriptural, because it is a truth from God.

We have seen in the last section that the Biblical principle is always 'Salvation is of the Lord'; 'The Lord
killeth, and maketh alive'.[6] Those whom the Lord, in his
mercy, purposed to save, are *known* of him[7] before they
could have done anything to merit God's foreknowledge.[8]
In the words of the Westminster Confession (III.5):

'Those of mankind that are predestinated unto life,
God, before the foundation of the world was laid, according to his eternal and immutable purpose, and the secret
counsel and good pleasure of his will, hath chosen in
Christ unto everlasting glory, out of his mere free grace
and love, without any foresight of faith and good works,
or perseverance in either of them, or any other thing in
the creature, as conditions or causes moving him there-
unto; and all to the praise of his glorious grace.'

There are three important things to be said about this
great doctrine of election:

Its source. It is God's purpose.[9] Spurgeon, preaching on

5. Jn. 6:65–66   6. Jonah 2:9; 1 Sam. 2:6; Ps. 37:39
7. 2 Tim. 2:19   8. Rom. 8:29; cf. Jn. 13:18
9. Eph. 1:9, 11; 2. Tim. 1:9; Rom. 8:28

Gal. 1:15, said: 'You will perceive, I think, in these words, that the divine plan of salvation is very clearly laid down. It begins, you see, with the will and pleasure of God. "When it pleased God . . ." The foundation of salvation is not laid in the will of man. It does not begin with man's obedience, and then proceed onward to the purpose of God, but here, in the purpose of God, is its commencement; here is the fountainhead from which the living waters flow.'

Its nature. It is unconditional. God set us apart for himself at the very beginning,[10] not according to his foresight of anything in us meriting our election (such as faith, or perseverance) which would, as we have said, entail salvation by our own works, but it was according to his love and mercy that he chose us for salvation.[11] The election of God is not a general ordination to eternal life of all who, as God foresees, will turn to him in faith; but it is a personal election, the *fruit* of which is always faith in the Lord Jesus Christ. 'As many as were ordained to eternal life believed.'[12] The *reason* for a man's election is simply that it pleased the Lord to have mercy upon him; for we read: 'For the children being not yet born, neither having done anything good or bad, that the purpose of God according to election might stand, not of works, but of him that calleth, it was said unto her [Rebecca], The elder shall serve the younger. Even as it is written, Jacob I loved, but Esau I hated.'[13] It might at this point be objected: Is not God unrighteous to appoint men to salvation in this way? 'God forbid!', says Paul, for 'I will have mercy on whom I have mercy, and I will have compassion on whom I have compassion. So then, it is

10. Eph. 1:4   11. Deut. 7:6; Rom. 11:5; Tit. 3:4–5
12. Acts 13:48   13. Rom. 9:11–13

not of him that willeth, nor of him that runneth, but of God that hath mercy.'[14] Far from being unrighteous, we have seen that God could righteously condemn every man, woman and child on this earth to eternal damnation, for all have deserved this end. Yet it pleased the Lord to have mercy upon some, to save and deliver some from this dreadful judgement – indeed, 'a great multitude, which no man could number'.[15] Such is the grace and mercy of our God!

The ground, then, of our salvation is our election. We are saved because it was his will. This absolute election, on a personal basis, to salvation, is something in which the believer ought to rejoice, and for which he ought humbly to thank God, as Jesus did,[16] and as Paul did.[17] 'Rejoice,' said the Lord Jesus, 'that your names are written in heaven.'[18] Here lies our assurance of salvation – if we had 'taken steps A, B and C' to become Christians, what guarantee would we have that we had taken those steps correctly? No! Our assurance is that God himself chose us from the beginning to be his; his Spirit bears witness with ours that we are the sons of God, and for this, and for no other reason, we can be sure that on the last Day, when the Son sits in judgement, and the Books are opened, our names will be found written in the Lamb's Book of Life, and he himself will say to us: 'Come, ye blessed of my Father, inherit the kingdom *prepared for you from the foundation of the world.*'[19]

Its purpose. It is, primarily, the glory of God.[20] But the election of saints is spoken of in Scripture as being but the first act by which God saves those on whom he has set his

14. Rom. 9:14–16   15. Rev. 7:9   16. Mt. 11:25
17. 2 Thess. 2:13   18. Lk. 10:20   19. Mt. 25:34
20. Eph. 1:6, 12

love. Those 'whom he *foreknew*' (that is, knew before as his chosen people; those on whom he had set his love in election to salvation[21]), 'he also *foreordained* to be conformed to the image of his Son;[22] whom he foreordained, them he also *called*' (by the effectual calling of the Holy Spirit, drawing them to himself); 'and whom he called, *them* he also *justified*' (by granting to the sinner saving faith in the death of Christ); 'and whom he justified, them he also *glorified*'.[23] So, the election of saints *ensures* their ultimate salvation as it ensures all the means thereto. Furthermore, Paul writes: 'We are his workmanship, created in Christ Jesus for good works, which God afore prepared that we should walk in them.'[24] It ensures for us the blessedness that comes from knowing that we are at peace with God.[25]

The most humbling thing that a Christian can know, and the truth that brings him to his knees before his Lord, is that his salvation is all of grace, that his election was solely of God's will and pleasure. We cannot tell why one dying thief, and not the other, went with Christ to paradise. We cannot tell why Peter was God's, while Judas was a reprobate. We cannot tell why we should have been born in places where the Gospel is preached, while millions never hear it. We can only say that it was the will of God that it should be so; that it was due to his great electing purpose. When we discover truths in Scripture that we from a human standpoint find hard, we should remember that the mystery lies in the will of God, which we can never fathom or know; that we are humbly to accept, without reservation, what God has revealed to us, not questioning what he has seen fit not to

21. 1 Pet. 1:2; Rom. 11:2   22. Phil. 3:21
23. Rom. 8:28–29   24. Eph. 2:10   25. Rom. 5:1

reveal;[26] and above all, that we should live to the praise of God in awareness that the purposes of God, not only in the salvation of sinners, but in all things, cannot be thwarted, but will surely come to pass. 'O the depth of the riches both of the wisdom and the knowledge of God! how unsearchable are his judgements, and his ways past tracing out! . . . Of him, and through him, and unto him are all things. To him be the glory for ever.'[27]

QUESTIONS AND OBJECTIONS CONSIDERED

God's election is based on his foreknowledge of who will believe: 'For whom he did foreknow, he also did predestinate . . .' (Rom. 8:29); 'Elect according to the foreknowledge of God the Father' (1 Pet. 1:2).

This objection springs from the mistaken idea that the foreknowledge spoken of in these verses is merely a passive cognition of what will come to pass. This is certainly the common usage in English; but the concepts of knowledge and foreknowledge in Scripture are far deeper (see IVF New Bible Dictionary, under 'predestination'). Let us take some other examples: 'Him (Jesus), being delivered by the determinate counsel and foreknowledge of God, ye have taken, and by wicked hands have crucified and slain'.[28] This foreknowledge is clearly active – almost equivalent to foreordination. 'God hath not cast away his people which he foreknew'.[29] Here, as in many other places in the Scriptures, to 'know' is used to express a deep personal relationship of love and choice. See also Mt. 7:23, 'I never knew you: depart from me, ye that work iniquity'; Jn. 10:14, 'I am the good shepherd, and

26. Deut. 29:29   27. Rom. 11:33–36   28. Acts 2:23
29. Rom. 11:2

know my sheep, and am known of mine'; Amos 3:2, 'You only have I known of all the families of the earth: therefore I will punish you for all your iniquities.'

The two verses quoted in the heading are misinterpreted thus: that God foresees that certain men will, of their own free-will, believe; and he therefore elects them to salvation. This is eisegesis, not exegesis. The verses themselves say nothing about foreknowledge of faith, or of anything else; nor does any phrase need to be supplied. The foreknowledge here spoken of refers to God's eternal love toward his elect. The same idea is expressed in Eph. 1:5 (if the RSV punctuation is adopted) 'He destined us *in love* to be his sons through Jesus Christ, according to the purpose of his will.'

We may finally show that this misinterpretation is directly contrary to the teaching of other Scriptures. Faith is always regarded as the result of election, the gift of God; never is God's election the ratification of man's choice. 'And as many as were ordained to eternal life believed.'[30] 'We give thanks to God always for you all . . . knowing, brethen beloved, your election of God. For our gospel came not unto you in word only, but also in power, and in the Holy Ghost, and in much assurance.'[31] 'But we are bound to give thanks alway to God for you, brethren beloved of the Lord, because God hath from the beginning chosen you to salvation through sanctification of the Spirit and belief of the truth.'[32] 'For unto you it is given in the behalf of Christ, not only to believe on him, but also to suffer for his sake.'[33] To Paul, then – and therefore to us also – faith is an evidence of election, and is one of the means ordained by God for the realization of

30. Acts 13:48   31. 1 Thess. 1:2–5   32. 2 Thess. 2:13
33. Phil. 1:29

his purposes. Indeed, it was for the salvation of the elect that Paul worked and suffered as he did.[34]

Careful reading of Ephesians ch. 1 and Romans ch. 9 makes it clear that God's election is absolutely independent of any condition whatever to be fulfilled by us.

God's election is of races and nations, not of individuals

The argument here is this: The election spoken of in the Bible is an election of nations. In the Old Testament dispensation, God chose Israel to be his people. Moreover, when Paul speaks of election in Romans ch. 9, he quotes (v. 13) from Malachi 1:2–3, where the prophet clearly has in view the *nations* of Israel and Edom, and not the individuals Jacob and Esau. The whole argument of Romans 9–11 is concerned with God's dealings with Israel as a nation; individuals are not the apostle's immediate concern.

So it is said; yet upon how little evidence will be apparent. We do not deny that God deals with nations; however, even here we must not forget – as God does not forget – that nations are composed of individuals. Our holy and just Lord does not raise up or cast down a nation irrespective of those individuals who make up the nation – as if he were to see them as mere statistics.

And although Scripture does speak of national election, it is only prejudice which can deny that in the vast majority of cases it is the election of *individuals* which is in view. Consider Mt. 24:24; Jn. 6:65; Jn. 15:6; Rom. 8:28–30, 33; 1 Cor. 1:26–31; Eph. 1:3–5, 11–12; 1 Thess. 1:4–5; 2 Thess. 2:13; 2 Tim. 2:10; Tit. 1:1; 1 Pet. 1:2; 2 Pet. 1:10. The reader who has looked up even

34. 2 Tim. 2:10

some of these verses will need no further demonstration that God chooses individuals unto salvation.

Yet this objection ought not to be left without a consideration of Paul's argument in Romans 9; for it is in this chapter that we see most clearly God's absolute sovereignty in election, and it would be damaging (though by no means fatal) to the Gospel of grace if it were to be shown that the election here spoken of is not of individuals, but of nations. Here is an outline of Romans, chapters 1 to 11, with particular detail in chs. 9 to 11.

Introduction (1:1–15)
Theme – the Gospel (1:16–17)
The sin of man and the judgement of God (1:18–32)
Jews and Gentiles alike guilty before God (2:1–3:20)
Justification by faith alone (3:21–4:25)
Christ's federal death for us, and its consequences (5:1–21)
Living under grace (6:1–23)
The Law and sin in the Christian life (7:1–25)
Living by the Holy Spirit (8:1–27)
The eternal security of the elect (8:28–39)
Objection: God's purposes for Israel seem to have failed, for she, the chosen people, has been cast off through unbelief (9:1–6a)
Answer: God's Word has *not* failed (9:6a)
Not all the natural children of Abraham are entitled to the promise:
   Example 1: Isaac, not Ishmael (9:7–9)
   Example 2: Jacob, not Esau (9:10–13)
God is not unrighteous, for his actions are sovereign (9:14–18)
No-one is entitled to question God's actions (9:19–21)

God demonstrates his power, wrath and mercy (9:22–23)

He has saved many of the Gentiles, and a remnant of Israel (9:24–30)

Explanation of Israel's unbelief: a contrast between justification by faith, and by works of the Law (9:31–10:5)

The Gospel of the free offer to all of salvation through faith (10:6–13)

The necessity of preaching the Gospel (10:14–21)

God has *not* cast Israel away, because:

(1) There is a *remnant* according to the election of grace, though the rest have been blinded (11:1–10)

(2) Israel's fall is not final. If their fall brought salvation to the Gentiles, how much more will their inclusion (11: 11–15)

Warning of the impartiality of God (11: 16–22)

(3) Israel shall be saved in the future (11:23–32)

Doxology: the unsearchable counsels and all-sufficiency of God (11:33–36)

Bearing this outline in mind, we see that Paul answers the charge against God that his promises to Israel have failed, by showing that in fact the promises were made to the nation as comprising elect *individuals*, e.g. Isaac and Jacob, and so the promises have been fulfilled to the elect remnant. Both the objections and Paul's replies of ch. 9:14–23 lose all their force if the discussion at this point is about nations. The fact that Paul quotes Malachi is no valid objection to this, for the prophet emphasises that God deals with the two nations according to his purposes for their individual parents. Luther's *Bondage of the*

Will should be read by all who are concerned to look into this question further.

God has stated that he has 'no pleasure in the death of the wicked; but that the wicked turn from his way and live' (Ezek. 33:11), and that he is 'not willing that any should perish, but that all should come to repentance' (2 Pet. 3:9).

The verse in 2 Peter is variously interpreted by commentators; some believe from the context ('longsuffering to *us*-ward') that it is the elect, and God's purpose to save all of them, which is spoken of; others, that the verse speaks of God's general desire that all men should repent, as in Ezek. 33:11.

If we adopt the more general interpretation, both verses teach much the same thing. God does not condemn the wicked gladly; he takes no pleasure in the pains of hell; rather, he is pleased when any sinner repents. Sinners who are finally lost are those who refuse to repent, and God manifests his holiness and justice in their punishment.

Why, then, it is asked, does not God elect all to salvation? We reply, why should he save any? Despite his goodness, men of their own accord universally refuse to repent. It is a mark of God's great mercy that he chooses to save some. No man has any right to question God's actions, as if we could judge the Lord of glory. We ought not to forget that God's purposes are not decided only by his mercy, but by his wisdom, in which he displays also his justice and power.

A right balance between God's sovereignty and man's responsibility is this: when a soul is lost, the fault is entirely its own; when a soul is saved, the glory is entirely God's.

As God's promises in the Gospel are universal, if he is sincere, the possibility of salvation cannot be restricted to a pre-chosen few. The Bible says: 'Whosoever shall call upon the name of the Lord shall be saved' (Rom. 10:13).

It is indeed a mystery which we cannot understand, that God sincerely offers the Gospel of salvation freely to all, while he has purposed to save only those whom he has chosen. Yet we are to believe it, for Scripture teaches both. Here is one of the paradoxes of the Word of God, which our feeble minds cannot resolve, but which our hearts receive by faith.

Yet we may comment that the sincerity of a promise is proved by its fulfilment. And the glorious fact is that these promises of God have in every single instance been found true. Everyone without exception who has called on the name of the Lord *has* been saved. Not one who has trusted in Christ has perished. There has never been a man who has *wanted* to come to Christ, who has found God's decree of election to be a barrier in the way.

The promises are universal in that no-one is excluded. But they are for those who come and take them. There are no gracious promises for those who *will not* believe. That is why we must beseech men to believe in Christ, so that they may take to themselves God's promises; and we know that they are enabled to do so as the Lord quickens their dead hearts and removes their unwillingness and stubbornness.

God cannot be just, if he unconditionally elects some to be saved, while others are passed over to be left to the consequences of their sins, which is eternal damnation.

If God is to be charged with dealing unjustly with men, it will have to be shown that men in some way *deserve* what God has been pleased to bestow upon some, and to deny to others – the eternal salvation of their souls. We have seen, however, that all men *deserve* only Satan's wages, which are eternal death and hell. God could, accordingly, be perfectly just in condemning all men to damnation. The Christian marvels, therefore, that, in contrast to the blackness of despair which he felt when it was shown to him that by the Law of God he stood condemned, and must inevitably hear the dreadful words 'Depart from me, ye cursed, into everlasting fire', another message shines out from God's Word: 'The Lord is gracious and full of compassion, slow to anger and plenteous in mercy',[35] in which is his hope. If a man is saved, it is because of God's mercy and grace – God's free and *unmerited* favour towards sinners; if a man is condemned, he is *justly* condemned for his own sins. Romans 6:23 is a universally beloved verse, because it contrasts what the sinner deserves with what he receives as a free gift from God. It is the prerogative, however, of the Giver to distribute the gift as he will,[36] and the justice of God would remain unimpaired, whether God had chosen not to save anybody, or to save all men.

The decrees of God, let it not be forgotten, are secret decrees, for 'who hath known the mind of the Lord?'[37] The mortal who dares question the counsels of the Most High, and blame God with injustice, is swiftly silenced by Paul: 'O man, who art thou that repliest against God? Shall the thing formed say to him that formed it, Why didst thou make me thus? Or hath not the potter a right over the clay, from the same lump to make one part a vessel unto honour, and another unto dishonour?'[38] The

35. Joel 2:13   36. Rom. 9:15   37. Rom. 11:34
38. Rom. 9:20–21

Christian is not the possessor of a salvation to which he has any right, but a debtor to the mercy of an all-wise and just Lord.

If the salvation of individuals depends on God's decree of election, then there is no motive for evangelism, since all whom God purposes to save will certainly be saved.

If for no other reason, the preaching of the Gospel is justified, at the most basic level, by the express command of the Lord Jesus Christ[39] and by the example and exhortations of the apostles. It was said by Moody that 'one plain text is as good as a thousand reasons'; God's counsels are secret; we do not know who is or who is not elect, except by observing signs of true regeneration – 'By their fruits ye shall know them' – amongst which are repentance and faith in the Lord Jesus Christ. The God-appointed means by which man comes to faith is the preaching of the Gospel;[40] and this, surely, is the proper answer to such an objection.

If we go further into the matter, we find that the conclusion which denies that there can be any reason to preach the Gospel is one of two alternatives which must follow logically from accepting as valid Reason's question, 'How can men be commanded to do what, by reason of their corrupt natures, they cannot do (i.e. repent, and believe the Gospel)?' The Arminian reply contends that since men *are*, in Scripture, commanded, then they must be able, whence there cannot be any unconditional decree of election; the reply with which we are here concerned denies that men *can* be commanded, and hence that there is any universal obligation to trust in Christ. From this specious argument is concluded that God is best

39. Mt. 28:19   40. Rom. 10:14

glorified by the Christian looking for the softest pillow he can find, while the eternal purposes are worked out, and the elect saved. Such are the excuses proffered by the so-called Hyper-Calvinists; it seems hardly necessary to say that their views are quite unscriptural and false; and that the logical conclusion would be total inactivity, with no preaching of the Gospel at all. The Scriptural answer is to say: Man can, and should, be commanded to do what by nature he cannot do. Indeed, the doctrine of election, far from being a hindrance to evangelism, ought to be the great encouragement for persevering in the preaching of the Gospel; since, through that preaching of the Gospel, all God's elect will indeed be saved, and God's cause will ultimately triumph, to his honour and glory. Finally, let it not be forgotten that the command of the Lord was: 'All power hath been given unto *me* . . . therefore, *go ye* . . .'[41] He commands us to be faithful in sowing; while God promises that of the seed sown, some will spring up to eternal life, and the weeping of sowing shall be turned into the rejoicing of reaping, as the roll of God's elect is filled up – as those whose names were from eternity written in the Book of Life find their salvation in Christ.

God loves all alike; hence there cannot be an unconditional decree of election to salvation

We must be clear about what we mean when we say that God loves all men alike. There are two senses to be given to the word 'loves' in this context; in one sense, God does indeed love all men; in the other, the Scriptures assert that he does not.

The distinction to be drawn is between God's love for

41. Mt. 28:18–19

men as their Creator, and his love for men as their Redeemer and Saviour. Inasmuch as God has created all men, and has pronounced his creation good, although now marred by sin, it can truly be said that God 'hates nothing that he has made', and he exhibits this love of Creator for what he has made by his upholding and providential care for his creatures. In this sense, God is the 'Saviour of all men'.[42] We must not lose sight of this important truth of the *universal* love of God, which we have mentioned in chapter 1. However, the Scriptures plainly teach that God's love as Redeemer is a *particular* love, manifested toward those upon whom he has set his love in their election, redemption, calling and glorification. It is a love from which nothing can separate God's own: 'For I am persuaded, that neither death, nor life, ... nor any other creature, shall be able to separate us from the love of God, which is in Christ Jesus our Lord.'[43] That God's redemptive love does not extend to all men is plainly taught in Malachi 1:2–3, this passage being cited by Paul in Romans 9:11–13: 'For the children being not yet born, neither having done anything good or bad, *that the purpose of God according to election might stand*, not of works, but of him that calleth, it was said unto her [Rebecca], The elder shall serve the younger; even as it is written, *Jacob I loved, but Esau I hated*.'

The whole truth lies, not at either of the Arminian or the Calvinistic extremes, but at both extremes together

The objection that the truth about the doctrines of the Gospel is a balance between 'Calvinism' and 'Arminianism' is a common one, stemming generally from a praiseworthy desire to arrive at the true Scriptural

42. 1 Tim. 4:10   43. Rom. 8:29–39; Eph. 5:25–27; *et al.*

balance between the doctrines emphasizing, on the one hand, the sovereignty of God, and on the other hand, the responsibility of man. The objection is frequently supported by appeals to the teaching of Charles Simeon ('Sometimes I am a high Calvinist, at other times a low Arminian, so that if extremes will please you, I am your man; only remember, it is not *one* extreme we are to go to, but *both* extremes'), and to the notion that the differences between Wesley and Whitefield resulted from the possession by each of but 'one half of the truth' concerning the doctrines of grace. The objection, then, is that the Calvinistic account of the matter, which we have put forward in this book, is one-sided; it is not that the account, in its positive aspects, is *wrong*, but that on its own it does not faithfully reflect the balance of Scripture, which, it is said, teaches the free-will of man as well as the sovereign election of God. Applications of this idea are often succinctly expressed: that one should be 'a Calvinist on one's knees, and an Arminian on one's feet'; that one should 'pray as if it all depended upon God, and work as if it all depended upon oneself'.

In answering this objection, we shall consider first, the absurdities to which it inevitably leads, and second, those parts of Scripture from which it claims to draw support.

First, then, the absurdities in which this teaching involves its adherents. If we follow it consistently, we must, on our knees, thank God for his eternal election, while on our feet informing sinners that salvation in fact rests upon their exercise of free-will. We must rejoice amongst ourselves that Christ's blood is sufficient of itself to redeem us from sin, while proclaiming to the world that, because Christ died for each and every man, it must be man's decision and exercise of faith that gives efficacy to the otherwise inoperative blood of the Redeemer. We are to believe that Christians are 'kept by the power of God . . . unto salvation', while indulging in frenzied 'follow-up' lest any who have truly believed should for ever fall away. In short, all that we say before God must be tire-lessly contradicted by all that we say before the world. That this should be the consequence of such opinions is hardly surprising, since, as we have endeavoured to show, Calvinism and Arminianism, far from being com-plementary, are irreconcilably opposed to each other. To assert the one set of doctrines is to deny, implicitly and explicitly, the other; and the claim that such contra-dictory 'truths' are to be found side by side in Holy Scripture, which is the Word of the God who cannot lie, must therefore be a claim that rests upon faulty exegesis of the text.

Secondly, let us look at some Scriptures which are often taken to show that 'Calvinistic' and 'Arminian' doctrines are taught side by side. It will be seen that, in all such cases, the true paradox is, not that between sovereignty and free-will, which would indeed lead to the Calvinist-Arminian antithesis, but between sovereignty and responsibility. We would refer, at this point, to the previous discussion on the difference between free-will and responsibility in Chapter 1.

Often quoted in this context is John 6:37. The first part of the verse speaks of the electing and predestinating purposes of the Father in giving a people to the Son, while the second part of the verse, as some claim, teaches that those who will not ultimately be cast out are those who have come to Christ as a result of their own free-will. It may readily be seen, however, that this interpretation is seriously at fault. No-one can come to the

Lord Jesus Christ of his own ability, for his nature is sinful and his will is depraved. All, therefore, who do come to Christ, come because they have been given to him by the Father; that they come willingly shows that their minds have begun to be illuminated by the Holy Spirit. Those who thus come will never be cast out, because the calling of God is *effectual*, that is, God's purposes are *realized*. And the realization of God's purpose in the giving spoken of in the first part of the verse, is the union of his elect with Christ: which is precisely what is expressed by the words 'will in no wise cast out' at the end of the verse.

The two-edged truth of sovereignty and responsibility is taught with clarity in Matthew 11:25–30. Here again, it is wrong exegesis to turn the gracious invitation of the Lord Jesus into a proof-text for free-will, and hence into an 'Arminian verse'. The invitation makes it clear that casting the burden of sin on to the Lord Jesus Christ is a *responsible* action; but the inference, 'responsibility, therefore free-will' is, as we have shown previously, purely philosophical, resting upon nothing in Scripture. Those who oppose the doctrines we have been putting forward with the charge that 'Calvinists are being more logical than Scripture' appear not to have noticed the beam that is in their own eye. The balance of Scripture, let it be said once again, is the balance between the sovereignty of God, and the responsibility of man, and these are truths which have always been taught by those known as Calvinists.

The paradox presented by these twin truths is analogous to that which necessarily belongs to the incarnation and also to that pertaining to the Christian's good works in this life. To see this will both illuminate the difficulty and set some minds at rest. When we see the glorious truth of the taking of the manhood into God, we begin to realize that, whenever God acts within man's terms of reference, there are bound to be paradoxical mysteries which we, possessing only finite minds and intelligence, are unable to comprehend. When we read Philippians ch. 2, we realize that we are not the first to see this connexion between the theology of the incarnation, and the truth of man's salvation by grace; vv. 1–11 concern the former, and vv. 12–13 the latter, a key 'therefore' connecting the two passages. Here is a classic statement of sovereignty and responsibility. Similarly, when we examine the theology of good works in the life of the Christian, we find the paradoxical teaching that good works are, in a sense, performed entirely by God, yet entirely by the Christian. The man with the withered hand (mentioned in the Gospel[44]) stretched forth his hand. It was most certainly he who did it; but the man's entire enabling was of the Lord Jesus Christ and him alone. Whenever Christ spoke the word of enablement no sufferer mentioned in the Gospels could ever plead inability to obey the command. In the Epistles we find Paul writing: 'For this I toil, striving with all the energy which he mightily inspires within me';[45] and again, 'But by the grace of God I am what I am, and his grace toward me was not in vain. On the contrary, I worked harder than any of them, though it was not I, but the grace of God which is with me.'[46]

To sum up, then: the objector may well be making a Scriptural point in his heart, but his terminology is misleading: for to equate the doctrines of sovereignty with

44. Mk. 3:1–5   45. Col. 1:29   46. 1 Cor. 15:10

'the Calvinistic truth', and the doctrines of responsibility with 'the Arminian truth', is to have misunderstood what Calvinism really is. The Calvinist is not embarrassed by those parts of Scripture which emphasize the responsibility of man; nor does he presume to recommend to the inspired writers that they alter some of their expressions that seem a little 'broad'. The Calvinist rejoices in the free offer of the Gospel to all men; for what preachers were more fond of pressing home to their hearers the responsibilities of the Gospel than the Calvinistic Puritans and their successors? We repeat, that it is hyper-Calvinism, and not Calvinism, that emphasizes the sovereignty of God at the expense of the responsibility of man. If, then, we are convinced of the truth of the doctrines popularly styled 'Calvinistic', let us be single-minded in preaching the Gospel with the courage of our convictions. God is not honoured by our holding firmly, or professing to hold firmly, to both opinions, any more than he is by our halting between them.

It is perhaps advisable to add that the use of the label 'Calvinism' does not imply that we believe these things because Calvin said them. John Newton commented on this misapprehension in a letter to a friend: 'I remember that, three or four years ago, I mentioned some part of the gospel truth to a gentleman who called on me here, and he answered, "If it is a truth, you are indebted for it to Calvin." As well might he have said, because Calvin had seen the sun, and has mentioned it in his writings, we build our knowledge of its light and influence upon his testimony. These are acknowledged throughout the world, whenever there is an eye to behold them. Here the courtier and the clown, the philosopher and the savage, are upon a level.'

If the doctrine of election is true, then it follows that all those who are not elect are infallibly predestined to condemnation, do what they may. The author of such a decree cannot be the God of mercy and love revealed in the Bible

The first thing to be said in connexion with the doctrine of reprobation here being spoken of is that the Scriptures tell us much more about God's decrees and purposes with regard to those being saved, than with regard to those who perish; the Gospel is good news, proclaiming to lost sinners an incomparable Saviour who delivers from the wrath to come. But since one of the principal objections to the doctrine of election is that it necessarily entails reprobation, it is important that the Scriptural teaching on the subject should be examined.

It is, as the objector rightly points out, a truth of logic that if God has purposed to save some, then he has also purposed not to save others. But not only is it a logical truth: it is also a Scriptural one. The Lord Jesus Christ thanked his Father that he had 'hid these things from the wise and understanding';[47] Paul declares that God 'hath mercy on whom he will have mercy, and whom he will he hardeneth', for 'hath not the potter power over the clay ... to make one vessel unto honour, and another unto dishonour?'[48] Peter says, of those 'which stumble at the word, being disobedient', that to this end 'they were appointed',[49] while Jude warns his readers of 'certain men crept in unawares, who were before of old ordained to this condemnation.'[50] It is clear, then, from Scripture, that God has decreed, or purposed, to do from eternity

47. Mt. 11:25   48. Rom. 9:18–22; cf. 2 Tim. 2:20
49. 1 Pet. 2:8; cf. 2 Pet. 2:9   50. Jude 4

what he actually does in time in regard to those who perish, as well as in regard to those who are saved.

The doctrine of reprobation may be stated thus: 'The rest of mankind God was pleased . . . to pass by, and to ordain them to dishonour and wrath for their sin' (Westminster Confession III, 7). It includes two distinct acts: that of *preterition*, a sovereign act of *passing by*, which is simply 'decreeing to leave – and in consequence leaving – men in their natural state of sin, – to withhold from them, or to abstain from conferring upon them, those special, supernatural, gracious influences, which are necessary to enable them to repent and believe', the result of which is that they continue in their sin and guilt; and that of *fore-ordination to damnation*, which is a judicial act by which God ordains such men to condemnation *on account of their sin*. It is very important to note that the punishment to which God has fore-ordained the non-elect is a *deserved* punishment: it is God's justice which requires that their sin be punished, and the decree is founded upon, and has reference to, their sin as a thing certain and contemplated. So it is that God is just, for the condemnation of a sinner is due to his own sin. There is little suggestion in Scripture that God's decrees of election and preterition contemplate men other than as in their fallen and sinful state, so that the sovereign act of preterition is a simple decree *not* to save, rather than a positive decree to damn a certain number arbitrarily (which would mean that men were *made* sinners to fit them for destruction).

The grace of God shines all the more brightly when we consider that, because all have sinned, all could justly have been passed by. Furthermore, it is worth noting that while an elect and justified sinner can receive assurance from the Holy Spirit of his eternal salvation, and that it is indeed God's will that he should, it is not the case that anyone can *know* himself to be fore-ordained to eternal damnation. Unregenerate men, in general, do not care; while the troubles of those that do are themselves generally evidence of a work of grace of the Holy Spirit, or of conviction prior to regeneration. While there is life, there is indeed hope; the offer of the Gospel is held out to all, and God's grace quickens the vilest of sinners.

In conclusion, some words of William Cunningham: 'Calvinists do not shrink from discussing the subject of reprobation, though, from its awful character, they have no satisfaction in dwelling upon it, and feel deeply the propriety of being peculiarly careful here not to attempt to be wise above what is written. . . . There is something about God's decrees and purposes, even in regard to those who perish, which can be resolved only into his own good pleasure, into the most wise and holy counsel of his will.'

The doctrine of election eliminates assurance

The argument here is that, because of God's decree of election, the believer can, on this earth, have no assurance of eternal salvation, since he must always be asking himself whether he is elect or reprobate. But, in fact, the exact opposite is the case! For the Christian, whose soul has been made free by the Son, with whose spirit the Holy Spirit bears witness that he is a son of God,[51] the grand reason, and the only reason, for his assurance, is that his salvation is entirely a work of grace, purposed by God from before the foundation of the world. He begins to realize that the good work begun in him, God will

51. Rom. 8:16

assuredly perfect to the day of Jesus Christ, and, with the knowledge that he is predestined to a glorious eternity in the presence of him who loved his soul, he is able, with assurance, to say:

> Yes, I to the end shall endure,
> As sure as the earnest is given.

Article XVII of the Church of England says:
'. . . The godly consideration of predestination, and our election in Christ, is full of sweet, pleasant and unspeakable comfort to godly persons, and such as feel in themselves the working of the Spirit of Christ, mortifying the works of the flesh, and their earthly members, and drawing up their mind to high and heavenly things, as well because it doth greatly establish and confirm their faith of eternal salvation to be enjoyed through Christ, as because it doth fervently kindle their love towards God. . . .'

Before leaving the subject, however, we must register our protest against the shallow teaching on assurance that is current amongst many evangelicals these days. The first thing that the young convert is generally told is: 'If you have taken the step, and decided to let Jesus Christ into your life, then he has come in. Rev. 3:20 says: "if any man . . . open the door, I will come in." ' Invariably accompanying this statement is the warning: 'Don't rely on your feelings.' Now, we believe the effect of such teaching to be very dangerous, and to be a perversion of the Scriptural doctrine that assurance is a gift from God. Sinners are told, on the basis of their decision for Christ, that they have eternal life, even if they have experienced no conviction of sin, and have not been brought to an end of their confidence in themselves. They do not expect to become changed people, because they have

never been taught that when God's Spirit performs a
work of grace, the result is a *new* creation. They do not
look for evidences, in terms of spiritual fruit, of their
regeneration, by which the Christian's calling and election are made sure, because they have been told that,
once they have made their decision, then no matter
what they feel like, and no matter what they do subsequently, they have been saved. Yet true God-given
assurance is always accompanied by an awareness of sin
being mortified; it is Scripture that commands us to
inspect our lives and to try ourselves, to see if we be in
the faith.[52] It is to be feared that, because of many who
have cried 'peace, peace; when there is no peace' with
God, because of no true work of grace in the heart, there
are people in our evangelical churches who sincerely believe themselves to be saved, because they cry 'Lord,
Lord', even though they do not the things their Lord
says. To such people, he will one day pronounce those
dreadful words: 'Depart from me, ye workers of iniquity.'
'Let him that thinketh he standeth take heed lest he
fall.'[53]

A final comment on the privilege of true assurance, by
Thomas Brooks:

'The being in a state of grace makes a man's condition
happy, safe, and sure; but the seeing, the knowing of
himself to be in such a state, is that which renders his life
sweet and comfortable. The being in a state of grace will
yield a man a heaven hereafter, but the seeing of himself
in this state will yield him both a heaven here and a
heaven hereafter; it will render him doubly blessed,
blest in heaven, and blessed in his own conscience.'

52. 2 Cor. 13:5   53. 1 Cor. 10:12

4

SALVATION ACCOMPLISHED

According to the divine plan of salvation, that is to say, the 'mystery which hath been hid from all ages and generations, but now hath ... been manifested to his saints'[1], the salvation of men is a triune work of Father, Son and Holy Spirit; the Father in election, and in sending his Son; the Son in redemption; and the Spirit in regeneration and sanctification. 'A plan', says C. Hodge, 'supposes: (1) the selection of some definite end or object to be accomplished; (2) the choice of appropriate means; (3) at least in the case of God, the effectual application and control of those means to the accomplishment of the contemplated end.' In this plan of salvation, the end, to which the death of the Lord Jesus Christ was the means, was the reconciliation with God of his people, through their redemption; and this redemption and reconciliation were infallibly secured at the cross of Calvary. Here it was that, in his plan to save those on whom he had been pleased to have mercy, God's elect were redeemed from sin, and their eternal salvation rendered certain.

The *purpose* of Christ's coming is clearly stated in Scripture. He came 'to seek and to save that which was lost'; he 'came into the world to save sinners'; he came to 'give his life a ransom for many',[2] that whosoever liveth and believeth in him should never die;[3] for these, who would believe in him, Christ gave himself 'that he might deliver us from this present evil world, according to the

1. Col. 1:26   2. Lk. 19:10; 1 Tim. 1:15; Mt. 20:28
3. Jn. 11:26

will of God and our Father'.[4] These, for whom he died, constitute his Church: he 'loved the church, and gave himself for it, that he might sanctify and cleanse it with the washing of water by the word, that he might present it to himself a glorious church, not having spot, or wrinkle, or any such thing; but that it should be holy and without blemish'.[5] As John Owen says, 'These last words express also the very aim and end of Christ in giving himself for any, even that they might be made *fit* for God, and brought nigh unto him.' So we read in Titus 2:14: 'He gave himself for us, that he might redeem us from all iniquity, and purify unto himself a peculiar people, zealous of good works.' In other words, all whom the Father had given to Christ,[6] those whom God had chosen for himself, the elect, Jesus Christ undertook to redeem from the curse of the Law by being made a curse for them,[7] by enduring for them the judgement of God which was their just due.

We are aware that the question 'For whom did Christ die?' is a much controverted one; yet we hold that the atonement described in Scripture is *particular* – the Lord Jesus Christ died specifically for the elect, as their representative and substitute, to secure their salvation. As Christ came into the world to *save* sinners, so we hold that the Cross makes certain the salvation of all those for whom Christ died. To hold that he died for all men leads either to the conclusion that all men are thereby saved (which Scripture denies), or that his death only made salvation possible for all, and not certain for some (which Scripture also denies), or that his death was not substitutionary at all (whereas Scripture plainly says that it

4. Gal. 1:4   5. Eph. 5:25–27   6. Jn. 10:29   7. Gal. 3:13

was). We shall consider these points later; for the moment, we want to justify our belief that Christ died for his Church, and not for the sins of each and every man:

Because particular atonement alone makes sense of the particular love of God the Father, and the particular calling and regeneration of the Holy Spirit. We have already stressed that God is sovereign in salvation. This means both that he is its Author, and that he grants it to whom he pleases, those of his own choice. God's election is particular: he, for his own glory, had mercy upon whom he would, and passed by the rest, leaving them to their condemnation. The Holy Spirit's calling is particular: he works in the hearts of those whom God has loved, bringing them to new birth, granting them repentance and faith, and obedience to the Word of God. So too is the atoning work of the one Mediator between God and man particular: he died for God's elect that they might be justified. 'He that spared not his own Son, but delivered him up for us all, how shall he not also with him freely give us all things? Who shall lay anything to the charge of God's elect? It is God that justifieth; who is he that shall condemn? It is Christ Jesus that died, yea rather, that was raised from the dead, who is at the right hand of God, who also maketh intercession for us.'[8]

Because the will of God is always accomplished. What he is pleased to purpose will surely come to pass. So, as it was the purpose of Christ's coming to save sinners, that is exactly what was achieved; and, by the cross, sinners are saved by being washed in the blood of Christ which was shed for them.

> *There is a fountain filled with blood,*
> *Drawn from Immanuel's veins;*

8. Rom. 8:32–34

And sinners, plunged beneath that flood,
Lose all their guilty stains.

No one who believes the teaching of Christ concerning the condemnation of unbelievers would deny that the benefits of Christ's death – redemption from sin, reconciliation with God, forgiveness – are enjoyed only by those who believe; for only these are reconciled to God,[9] justified in his sight and sanctified,[10] and adopted into his family.[11] But since these things were achieved at the cross, and partaken of by a certain group of people (who believe), so we maintain that they were intended for those by whom they are possessed (the elect), since otherwise the purposes of God in sending his Son become no more than pious hopes and vain wishes for the salvation of the world, for all mankind. The Bible sets forth a redemption that is *personal*. 'The Son of God loved me, and gave himself for me'[12] is the testimony of every born-again soul, because Jesus died that that soul might live.

Because the Church is the Bride of Christ,[13] whom he loves with an everlasting love. Here again, we see the forcefulness and deep meaning of the metaphor of marriage. The essence of the bride-bridegroom relationship is that the groom knows and loves the bride; so, when the Lord Jesus loved the Church, and gave himself for it, he was giving himself for a bride whom he already *knew* and cared for.[14] By his death, he delivered his bride from darkness, and brought her into the banqueting-house, the place of rejoicing, where the union takes

9. Rom. 5:10; Eph. 2:16 ff.
10. Heb. 9:14; 13:12; 1 Jn. 1:7; Eph. 5:25–27
11. Gal. 4:4–5; Rom. 8:15   12. Gal. 2:20
13. Rev. 21:2   14. Jer. 31:3; Eph. 5:25; Song 2:2

place.[15] If Christ died for all men, then he has a bride whom he does not know, and cannot therefore love with the particular love that every bridegroom has for his spouse.

Because God is just. All sin must be punished, but he does not require it to be punished twice over. The Lord Jesus Christ died as our representative, inasmuch as those for whom he died were themselves condemned, in his person, at the cross. When he died, they died in him and in his resurrection they passed from death to life.[16] To all those who died, in Christ, on the cross, there is no more condemnation,[17] because they have already been condemned; their Substitute 'became sin' for them. God cannot, therefore, condemn a man for whom Christ died, for Christ paid the penalty for his sin once and for all. But, as all those, like Judas, who are condemned, are not saved, then Christ cannot have died for them, for God does not demand two payments for a man's sin, when, under the New Covenant, Christ's blood was accepted as a full, perfect and sufficient sacrifice for that sin. If any one man perishes for whom Christ died, then God is unjust indeed. Jesus came to *save* sinners, and that is exactly what he does, by his death.

> The terrors of law and of God
> With me can have nothing to do;
> My Saviour's obedience and blood
> Hide all my transgressions from view.

It is our claim that this doctrine of particular, or, as it is often misleadingly termed, 'limited' atonement, alone does justice to the free saving grace of God, and is the

15. Song 2:4; Col. 1:13; Mt. 25:10   16. 2 Cor. 5:14–17
17. Rom. 8:1

only atonement to be found in his Word. If we say that Christ died for all men, 'then we must also say that "Christ died that any man might live if . . ." and then follow certain conditions of salvation.' Yet, the grace of God is free[18] and unconditionally given to helpless sinners. 'Christ's death ensured the calling and keeping – the present and final salvation – of all whose sins he bore. That is what Calvary meant, and means. The cross *saved*; the cross *saves*.'

This, the saving-power of the blood of the Lamb, is why the cross stands at the very centre of the Christian faith.

QUESTIONS AND OBJECTIONS CONSIDERED

There are many verses which declare that Christ died for the world, or for all men

It is true that Scripture says that Christ died for the world.[19] It also says that he died for all,[20] though it is noteworthy that the expression 'all men' is found only once in connexion with the death of Christ[21] – in all other cases where it is found in English versions, the word 'men' has been supplied by the translators.

It might seem that these texts prove the case for universal redemption. But this is to take a superficial view of the question; and we shall attempt to show that the case is by no means proved – that, on the contrary, these verses may be legitimately understood so as to agree with

18. Rom. 3:24; 6:23
19. Jn. 1:29; 3:16; 4:42; 6:51; 2 Cor. 5:19; 1 Jn. 2:2; 4:14
20. Is. 53:6; Jn. 12:32; 2 Cor. 5:14–15; 1 Tim. 2:6; Heb. 2:9
21. Rom. 5:18

the Biblical evidence already adduced for particular redemption. There are three lines of argument which we shall bring to bear: first, that the terms 'world' and 'all', though universalistic in form, are very frequently used in Scripture with limited or indefinite reference; second, that a more detailed exegesis of these verses in context shows that universalism is not intended; and third, that a universalistic interpretation contradicts the Scriptural witness to the nature of Christ's death.

The meanings of the word 'world' in Scripture are briefly as follows:

1 The habitable earth, or, more generally, the created universe. [Job 34:13; Ps. 24:1; 90:2; Mt. 13:38; 26:13; Acts 17:24; Eph. 1:4; (1 Tim. 1:15); *et al.*]

2 The inhabitants of the earth.
   (i) Each and every individual. [Rom. 3:6, 19]
   (ii) Men in general, or many. [Mt. 24:14; Lk. 2:1; Jn. 7:4; 12:19; 16:8; 17:21; Rom. 1:8; 10:18; 1 Cor. 4:9; Col. 1:6]

3 Evil.
   (i) Wicked men, as opposed to God's people. [Is. 13:11; Jn. 7:7; 14:17, 22; 15:19; 17:9, 25; 1 Cor. 6:2; 11:32; Heb. 11:38; 1 Jn. 5:19; Rev. 13:3]
   (ii) In general, the corrupt and Satanic condition of men. [Mt. 18:7; Jn. 14:30; 18:36; Rom. 12:2; 1 Cor. 2:12; 7:31, 33; Gal. 1:4; Eph. 2:2; 6:12; Col. 2:8; Jas. 1:27; 1 Jn. 2:15–17; 4:5]

The word 'all' has also different meanings:

1 All of all sorts. [Lk. 24:25; Acts 10:36; 20:27; Rom. 5:18a; 1 Cor. 7:17]

2 All of some sorts. [Lk. 4:13; Rom. 5:18b; 1 Cor. 8:1; 15:22; Eph. 4:6]

3 Some of all sorts. [Mt. 9:35; Mk. 11:32; Lk. 11:42; 18:12; Acts 2:17; Rom. 14:2; 1 Cor. 1:5; 1 Tim. 2:1–3, 8]

When Christ is said to have died for 'the world' or for 'all', those who wish to demonstrate universal redemption must prove that 'world' is used in sense 2(i), and 'all' in sense 1. It is plain that this is by no means evident on the grounds of usage. The question is not, 'what is the ordinary sense of "world" or "all" in English?' (for the Bible was not written in English); but rather one must find out the meaning of a word in any particular verse by studying how that word is used elsewhere in Scripture, and in its context.

Having demonstrated that the verses under consideration need not assert universal redemption, we now turn to the second line of argument: exegesis of these verses in context. Lack of space necessitates that only a few of the more important examples be considered.

John 3:16. 'For God so loved the world, that he gave his only begotten Son, that whosoever believeth on him should not perish, but have eternal life.' The purpose of this so well-known verse is to declare the greatness of the love of God. At once we see the inadequacy of the view that 'the world' means each and every man. For then our attention is concentrated on the vast number of individuals who compose the world; but, great as this is by earthly standards, it is as nothing by which to measure the love of God. Moreover, on this view, what has God's love done for 'the world'? Only the opening of a way of salvation before it: whereas the very next verse asserts that God's purpose is far greater than that – it is actually to save the world. Are we to say, then, that 'the world' here means, in effect, 'the elect'? Although this view has much to commend it, it hardly seems to do justice to the concept of 'the world'. And, when we see also that the term is comprehensive, that the world is envisaged as a whole, it seems that we ought to understand 'world' in its primarily *moral* sense: it is that corrupt society of humanity, which is under Satan's power, and which is at enmity with God. That this sense (3(ii) in the table given above) is the one most appropriate here is confirmed by the fact that the world is viewed as perishing; and so, although Christ could have come to judge the world, he came rather to save the world. The greatness of God's love is measured by this: that he loves the corrupt and sinful world so much that he sent, not judgement, but salvation. So by 'the world' here is meant humanity, not quantitatively, but qualitatively. If one insists on asking whether all men are intended, we must reply that they are not, for God's love is here set forth as of saving efficacy; yet the objects of his love are described not as the elect, but as sinners – to emphasize the mercy and grace of the love of God.

1 John 2:1–2. 'And if any man sin, we have an Advocate with the Father, Jesus Christ the righteous: and he is the propitiation for our sins; and not for ours only, but also for the whole world.' It must certainly be admitted that these verses are quite consistent with universal atonement; and that, if that were the overall teaching of Scripture, no more would need to be said. But it is also plain that this statement of the apostle John may be understood compatibly with limited atonement, and that within the scope of his argument there are several reasons why he should have used the expression 'the whole world', without implying at all that Christ's propitiation, any more than his Advocacy, extends to the sins of each individual man. John here contemplates the glory of the work of Christ, who is not only the means of propitiation, but in himself the embodiment of propitiation; and so proclaims him, with praise and wonder, in *three ways* the propitiation 'for our sins; and not for ours only, but also for the whole world'. First, Christ's propitiation is universal in its *extent* – effective not just for the Jews, or for the believers to whom John writes, but for all in every nation the world over who come into saving union with him. Secondly, Christ is the *only* propitiation for sin: 'neither is there any other name under heaven, that is given among men, wherein we must be saved'.[22] And thirdly, Christ's propitiation endures *for ever*: always effective 'if any man sin', and powerful for believers of every age. This is sufficient reason for the expression 'also for the whole world'.

Hebrews 2:9. 'But we behold . . . Jesus, because of the suffering of death crowned with glory and honour, that by the grace of God he should taste death for every (man).' Are we to take 'every man', or 'every one', to refer to all men without exception? Let the context decide. The writer is speaking of the 'many sons' being brought 'unto glory'; of 'they that are sanctified'; of Christ's 'brethren'; of 'the children which God hath given [him]'.[23] There is no reason to extend the reference of verse 9 beyond that of the subsequent verses.

We conclude our discussion and re-emphasize our previous points by a third line of argument: that the nature of Christ's death as described in Scripture – even in the very verses under consideration – is such as to rule out a universalistic view of the atonement. Did Christ die to make men salvable, or to save them? Has he

22. Acts 4:12   23. verses 10–13

'obtained eternal redemption',[24] or has he made all men redeemable? The saving power and effectiveness which the concepts of salvation, redemption, propitiation, etc. imply may not be watered down. If Christ has given himself a ransom for every individual man, then every man must be saved; for God cannot require the ransom payment twice – from Christ and from the sinner also. Since it is apparent from Scripture that not all men are saved, and it is equally apparent that the atonement is effective, a universalistic view, though initially plausible from these few verses, may not be held.

Limited atonement limits the grace of God

We have referred to this doctrine as 'Particular Atonement' and not by its more common name of 'Limited Atonement', in order to avoid giving this wrong impression. But of course the objection is not answered by changing the name of the doctrine! We are content to say, with C. H. Spurgeon:

'We are often told that we limit the atonement of Christ, because we say that Christ has not made a satisfaction for all men, or all men would be saved. Now, our reply to this is, that, on the other hand, our opponents limit it: we do not. The Arminians say, Christ died for all men. Ask them what they mean by it. Did Christ die so as to secure the salvation of all men? They say, "No, certainly not." We ask them the next question – Did Christ die so as to secure the salvation of any man in particular? They answer "No." They are obliged to admit this, if they are consistent. They say "No. Christ has died that any man may be saved if" – and then follow certain conditions of salvation. Now, who is it that

24. Heb. 9:12

limits the death of Christ? Why, you. You say that Christ did not die so as infallibly to secure the salvation of anybody. We beg your pardon, when you say we limit Christ's death; we say, "No, my dear sir, it is you that do it." We say Christ so died that he infallibly secured the salvation of a multitude that no man can number, who through Christ's death not only may be saved, but are saved, must be saved and cannot by any possibility run the hazard of being anything but saved.'

There is only one sense in which it may be said that we limit the grace of God: that is, that we deny that all men individually will be saved. And in this sense, we are not ashamed to put the same limits on grace that God himself has put, for Universalism is quite contrary to the Scriptures.

Particular atonement would invalidate the universal promises of the Gospel

God's promises are indeed sincere, and given to all. But they express the connexion between faith and salvation, and demonstrate the duty of all men everywhere to repent and believe; they do not express God's purpose to save all men. For the promises of the Gospel are conditional – on willingness to come, on repentance, on belief, on calling on the name of the Lord –; but God's purposes are unconditional.

There is thus no contradiction, either in logic, or in Scripture, or in fact, between particular atonement and God's universal offer of salvation.

The atonement cannot be spoken of in numerical terms

It is said that we who believe in a particular atonement are trying to tie down to finite terms what is infinite. The atonement was a redemptive act so great that it is meaningless to think of atonement being made for some and not for others.

It is puzzling to know how to answer an assertion of meaninglessness. A statement such as 'The kryuxis has a red tail' is meaningless because the word 'kryuxis' has no defined content. A statement containing only ordinary English words may also be meaningless; e.g. 'The spaniel splintered in the sunshine', where there is an incongruity between the subject 'the spaniel' and the verb 'splintered'.

The doctrinal statement 'Christ died for the elect, and not for the rest of mankind' can only be meaningless if there is an incongruity between 'died for' and the *limited* object 'the elect'. This must depend on the meaning of Christ's death. If he died only as an *example*, it is true that the above statement would be meaningless, for an example is by its nature universally valid. But Scripture also teaches that Christ died as a ransom, as a *substitute*, as a propitiation for sin. These are personal and individual transactions, which are limited by the intention of the one who carries out the transaction – this is so in the affairs of men, where these concepts originated, and is equally so in that great act of the accomplishment of redemption.

Everyone will admit that Christ's death is limited in some ways: he did not die for the evil angels, or for the animals, or for inanimate creation – for these there is not, neither can there be, any reconciliation with God (which is the purpose of the death of Christ). There is, therefore, no reason why it should be meaningless to limit the atonement to those whom God has actually purposed to save.

Far from being meaningless, particular atonement is set forth in the types of the legal dispensation. For example, on the day of atonement, Aaron and his high priestly successors were to make an atonement for the children of Israel for all their sins.[25] Here was a particular atonement, made for God's chosen people, and not for the heathen nations round about. The Passover lamb was similarly slain for the Israelites, not for the Egyptians: it was those individuals for whom the blood had been shed who found they were under no condemnation.

The atonement is sufficient for all.

This we do not deny. Owen says: 'The value, worth, and dignity of the ransom which Christ gave himself to be, and of the price which he paid, was infinite and immeasurable; fit for the accomplishing of any end and the procuring of any good, for all and every one for whom it was intended, had they been millions of men more than ever were created.'

The atonement is sufficient in itself for all those for whom it is intended. If the Lord had intended to save every man, the atonement would be sufficient for it. But in fact he has designed and made this atonement specifically for those whom he actually intends to save by it.

If the atonement is particular, then evangelists can no longer preach that 'Christ died for you*'.*

This is true, and we believe such a statement to be quite without warrant when addressed to sinners in general. It is no part of the Biblical Gospel, or of the preaching of the apostles, to say 'Christ died for *you*' – an

25. Lev. 16:34

assertion which is presumptuous on the part both of the one who makes it and of the one who accepts it, who yet may not have saving faith. As Dr. J. I. Packer says:

'The fact is that the New Testament never calls on any man to repent on the ground that Christ died specifically and particularly for him. The basis on which the New Testament invites sinners to put faith in Christ is simply that they need him, and that he offers himself to them, and that those who receive him are promised all the benefits that his death secured for his people. What is universal and all-inclusive in the New Testament is the invitation to faith, and the promise of salvation to all who believe. . . . The gospel is not, "believe that Christ died for everybody's sins, and therefore for yours", any more than it is, "Believe that Christ died only for certain people's sins, and so perhaps not for yours." The gospel is, "Believe on the Lord Jesus Christ, who died for sins, and now offers you himself as your Saviour." This is the message which we are to take to the world. We have no business to ask them to put faith in any view of the extent of the atonement; our job is to point them to the living Christ, and summon them to trust in him.'

Paul was able to say 'The Son of God loved me, and gave himself for me',[26] and every true believer who has received assurance of his salvation may also say this. Why? Because he knows God has *saved* him. It is the zenith, not the beginning, of faith to appropriate to oneself this verse. No-one who has not *first* repented and trusted in Christ to save him, may legitimately believe that Christ died for him personally.

26. Gal. 2:20

5

THE HOPE OF GLORY

Because our salvation is entirely God's work, we can be assured that 'He which began a good work in [us] will perfect it until the day of Jesus Christ'.[1] The promise of the Lord Jesus, which is sure, because God's Word is sure, and stands for ever, is that all who come to him, he will never cast out – precisely because those who come to him have been given to him of the Father.[2] This is the precious truth of the *final perseverance* of the saints – that all who have been born again shall be eternally saved. The Biblical truth is not so much one of the 'eternal security of believers', which implies that a man is saved only for as long as he is able to 'hold on' to God by faith, or that there is nothing for the believer to do *but* believe; the promises of eternal life in the Scriptures are given to those who shall endure, who are faithful unto death, who persevere, who watch and pray;[3] and the expression 'final perseverance' reminds the Christian that these things, like the first act of repentance and faith, are gifts from God. It is by the grace of God that the saints persevere to the end.[4] The doctrine that a man who has been saved by the blood of Christ, who has been born of the Spirit of God, and in whom that Spirit dwells, could ever fall from grace, is one of the most injurious ever invented by Satan. The Word of God flatly denies it; for Christ will

1. Phil. 1:6
2. Jn. 6:37; cf. 1 Pet. 1:5; Heb. 6:17–19; Prov. 4:18
3. Mt. 24:13; Rev. 2:10; Jas. 1:12; Mt. 25:13
4. Ps. 37:24

never part with the soul for which he paid so dearly with his precious blood. Backslide, like Peter, a man may; leave his first love, like the church at Ephesus, he may; grieve the Holy Spirit he may; but be forsaken by God he cannot; for he has been for ever united with the Lord Jesus, in an embrace that can never be broken.[5] His sins are covered by the blood of the Lamb; the Lord God sees us in our Saviour rather than in our sin.

Scripture makes it clear that saints are elected to salvation through *sanctification*,[6] and that the same Holy Spirit who works regeneration also works sanctification[7] in the life of the believer. 'Unsanctified Christian', 'Christian who does not have the Holy Spirit', 'Christian who has only accepted Christ as Saviour, and not as Lord', are all contradictions in terms; for Paul clearly writes to the Christians at Corinth, to whom he confessed he could not speak as spiritual, but as carnal,[8] that they (of all people) were sanctified,[9] that they had received their new life from the Holy Spirit,[10] that they were temples of the Holy Spirit,[11] and that, if they were born of God's Spirit, then Jesus Christ was their Lord[12] as well as their Saviour. Sanctification, as much as election, regeneration, justification, and so on, is the work of the Lord, and every one who partakes of these benefits must also partake of sanctification, and is a saint in the true sense – a sanctified one, separated to God's service. By God's grace, saints are able to live the consecrated lives of discipleship required of them, because they are being lived in the strength of the Lord Jesus Christ. As those who have been set free from

5. Song 2:16; 8:7   6. 2 Thess. 2:13; 1 Pet. 1:2
7. Ezek. 36:27; Rom. 15:16   8. 1 Cor. 3:1, 3
9. 1 Cor. 6:11   10. 2 Cor. 3:3   11. 1 Cor. 6:19
12. 1 Cor. 12:3

bondage to sin,[13] they are able both to will and to do things that please God, because such works spring from a living faith in Christ; to work out their own salvation, to mortify the deeds of the body, to seek holiness, without which no man shall see the Lord, and to abstain from sin.[14] It is by the fruits of the Spirit that Christians are known to be God's children – those sweet fruits of obedience to the Word of God which must follow when the Holy Spirit dwells within a man; for, if any man is in Christ, he is a *new creature*.[15] Just as the Ethiopian cannot change his skin, neither the leopard his spots, so neither can an unsaved man attain to sanctification – whether he be 'committed', 'decided', or anything else which, as experience has shown, unregenerate man *can* attain to. It is common to explain away the fact that someone who has 'professed' conversion does not show any evidence of a change of heart, by saying that he is 'carnal'; while if he subsequently falls away, it is said that he is only backsliding, and all will soon be well. Scripture knows nothing of Christians who show no marks of sanctification, and falling away is a sure sign that such people never truly belonged to Christ.[16] One of the evidences of true sanctification is the 'continual and irreconcilable war, the flesh lusting against the Spirit, and the Spirit against the flesh; in which war, although the remaining corruption may for a time much prevail, yet, through the continual supply of strength from the sanctifying Spirit of Christ, the regenerate part doth overcome; and so the saints grow in grace, perfecting holiness in the fear of God (Westminster Confession, XIII, 2–3).

13. Jn. 8:36
14. Phil. 2:12–13; Rom. 8:13; Heb. 12:14; 1 Pet. 2:11
15. 2 Cor. 5:17   16. 1 Jn. 2:19

The glorious work of our salvation finds its completion in the second coming of the Lord Jesus Christ; then takes place the resurrection and glorification of the saints, thereafter to be for ever in the presence of the One who loved them and washed them from their sins.[17] Our glorification is certain;[18] and so it is that the saints fight the good fight of faith here below, strengthened by the knowledge that, because God directs all things after the counsel of his own will, his cause will ultimately triumph. So too, they watch and pray for that great day when death will flee in the face of the glory of the Lord Jesus Christ, when sorrow and sighing shall be no more, when they shall have everlasting joy, when they shall be with *him* for ever.

He which testifieth these things saith, yea: I come quickly. Amen: come, Lord Jesus.

QUESTIONS AND OBJECTIONS CONSIDERED

There are several passages which speak of believers falling away: 1 Cor. 8:11; Rom. 14:15; Heb. 6:4–8; Heb. 10: 26–31; 2 Pet. 2:1, 20–22

1 Cor. 8:11 and Rom. 14:15 are similar, and may be considered together. Paul exhorts that no cause of stumbling should be put before a weak brother. He explains that this is a sin, because its natural tendency is to cause the weak Christian to fall into sin, and to perish, which would be to frustrate the purpose of Christ in dying for him. It is not implied that this could actually happen; it is sufficient that, without God's intervention, it would happen. When Saul threw a javelin at David,[19] he in-

17. 1 Thess. 4:16–18; Rev. 7:14–17   18. Jn. 6:39–40
19. 1 Sam. 18:11

tended to kill him, and was guilty, because the intrinsic tendency of his action was to kill; yet it was not possible that he should succeed, for God had anointed David to be King over Israel.

Of the passages in Hebrews there are several possible interpretations. (1) Despite the strong expressions used in Hebrews 6:4–5 and 10:29, many commentators (e.g. Calvin, Owen) believe these passages to refer to professing Christians who have been enlightened, and have received many of the privileges of God, and yet who are not true believers (cf. King Saul or Judas). They claim that nothing is here said which *must* necessarily be understood of the regenerate. (2) Others consider that it is more natural to understand true believers to be spoken of, but that the cases are hypothetical, intended as a warning. When Paul warned the sailors to stay in the ship,[20] he explained that unless they stayed they could not be saved. Yet he knew, and had previously told them,[21] that they would be saved. It was still necessary to warn them not to do what he knew they would not do. God ordains not only ends, but also the means to those ends. The view that these passages in Hebrews 6 and 10 are hypothetical, is supported by 6:9, in which the writer makes it clear that he does not mean that this will happen to any of his readers. 10:26 begins 'If we sin ...' and may therefore also legitimately be understood as hypothetical. (3) The interpretation that these passages speak of the actual apostasy of true believers, while possible from these alone, is not necessary, as we have shown, and contradicts the clear testimony of other passages.

The most probable explanation of 2 Pet. 2:1 is that Peter is speaking of these false teachers according to the

20. Acts 27:31   21. vv. 22–26

terms of their own profession. They claimed that Jesus was their Lord and Redeemer, and were therefore considered as his people by the church. Their denial of Jesus Christ under these circumstances aggravated their condemnation. In general, Scripture ascribes to those in the fellowship of the church that which is strictly applicable only to those who are in fact elect and redeemed.

2 Pet. 2:20 speaks of a reformation from the ways of the world, which may be merely outward, and this is confirmed by verse 22. The sow that is washed is outwardly clean – but it is still a *sow*: its nature is unchanged, and it is for this reason that it returns to wallow in the mire. The unregenerate man may, by close contact with the Gospel, reform his conduct and behave like a Christian; but his nature is the same, and he inevitably returns to his sinful ways.

God will not force me to continue to be a Christian against my will

This objection is similar to the objection that it is possible to resist the Holy Spirit, and embraces a contradiction; for, when the Spirit of God brings a soul to new birth, a new principle is planted within that person – the work of God within him 'both to *will* and to do his good pleasure'; anyone who does not will to continue to confess Christ, and who does not want to become like him – who looks back and falls away – can never have truly belonged to the Lord Jesus Christ, and is not an inheritor of the Kingdom of God. That, in the continual warfare between the flesh and the Spirit, the old nature may for a season gain the upper hand, and the believer backslide, is plain, both from Scripture and from Christian experience; yet the regenerate nature, the will and desire to please God and to abide in Christ, can never be vanquished, and one day will overcome all, by the grace of God, who restores the soul, and who freely and abundantly forgives. Peter, the backsliding believer, wept tears of godly sorrow and repentance, when he saw his sin; Judas, the apostate, filled with remorse when he saw what his action had led to, went out and committed the sin which admits of no repentance, by hanging himself; the one, who had been granted saving faith in the Lord Jesus, restored, – the other, who had never possessed true faith, cast down.

The doctrine of the final preservation of Christians leads logically to the supposition that the saved can live as they please, since they can never be lost

This is precisely how those professing Christians known as antinomians reasoned; their licentious and utterly immoral behaviour brought shame and dishonour upon the name of Christ, and caused many saintly men to react sharply against any doctrine teaching eternal and assured salvation for anybody on this earth. Like the previous objection, this one embraces the same contradiction, and ignores the fact that the Christian, the true believer, is a *changed* person – he no longer desires the things the world desires, nor reasons as the world reasons; his desire is to become holy, to glorify God by walking in the steps of his Master, to hate sin in all its forms, and to flee from it and from all occasions of temptation, for all that his soul is worth. The logic which infers the legitimacy of immorality from the truth of final perseverance is phoney logic – it ignores the fact that the same Spirit who preserves also *sanctifies* and transforms. 'Without holiness, no man shall see God'; no-one who uses his 'knowledge' of eternal salvation as a cloak for mischief can have any reason to believe that he is one of God's elect. 'Let him that thinketh he standeth take heed lest he fall.'

6

ANOTHER GOSPEL

Many who have read thus far may well feel that they do not recognize it, in emphasis or in substance, as the gospel with which they are familiar. It is our contention that this is a real and basic difference, and that it is the difference between the Biblical Gospel of our Lord Jesus Christ and a man-made substitute gospel. To substantiate this claim, we must examine the modern gospel and compare it with Scripture – for our final authority must be the Scriptures alone, which contain many warnings against false gospels.[1] If we are to be true to our duty to 'test everything; hold fast what is good',[2] we must test all formulations of the gospel against that one true Gospel which is revealed in the Word of God. This is the aim of this chapter.

If the gospel commonly preached today is indeed found to be unscriptural, it follows that much of modern evangelicalism has gone astray on doctrines which are not just of secondary importance, but are at the heart of the Christian faith. This is not a welcome conclusion, but we must not avoid it for that reason. In the last few years the Lord has laid a desire for the revival of true, deep, vital and powerful Christianity on the hearts of many; it may well be that the recovery of the purity of the Gospel will, by the grace of God, lead to a healing of the many ills and weaknesses of the evangelical churches, and to a demonstration of the Holy Spirit's power amongst us

1. Gal. 1:6–9; 1 Tim. 6:3, 20; 2 Tim. 1:13–14; *et al.*
2. 1 Thess. 5:21

both in the growth in grace of believers, and in the salvation of the lost.

We proceed therefore to consider the manner in which the way of salvation is frequently preached these days. We are reluctant to say it, yet we are convinced that much modern preaching which purports to be evangelical falls short of Scriptural teaching, and has little in common with the example of the Master Evangelist, the Lord Jesus Christ himself. How would much modern evangelistic preaching and writing answer the question of the rich young ruler, 'What must I do to inherit eternal life?'? The following answer (found in one much-used evangelistic booklet) is probably typical: 'If I am to benefit from Christ's death I must take three simple steps, of which the first two are preliminary, and the third so final that it will make me a Christian . . . I must believe that I am, in God's sight, a helpless sinner, that is, I must *admit my need*: I must *believe that Christ died for me*; I must *come to him*, and claim my personal share in what he did for everybody.' Under the third and final step is explained how the willing sinner must 'open the door of his heart to Christ', the Christ who waits patiently outside the door, until I open it to him.

It is undeniable that such an answer, or something like it, is frequently presented today, and those who teach such a method probably justify it by claiming that it includes the central doctrines of the Gospel – repentance, faith, conversion, substitutionary atonement, the sinfulness of man, and so on. If someone 'takes the step', and later questions the validity of his conversion, he is assured that '*you* took a simple step; *you* committed yourself to Jesus Christ; but *then* God performed a stupendous

miracle. He gave you new life; you were born again. . . .'
(our italics). The concluding advice is often given: 'Tell
somebody today what you have done.' This answer bears
little resemblance to Jesus' reply to the rich young ruler.[3]

The following is a summary of some of the basic doctrines or presuppositions of this modern gospel:

The unregenerate man is regarded as capable of repenting and believing.

The demand to believe that Christ died for *your* sins is
based on the doctrine that Christ died for the sins of every
man individually.

Committing oneself to Christ, or deciding for him, or
coming to him, is presented as an act which the sinner can
do as he wills at any time, i.e. as an act of free-will.

Although God may be said to have taken the initiative
in a general sense by sending Christ to die to make salvation possible, in any particular conversion it is the sinner
who takes the initiative by coming to Christ, and it is
God who responds.

Now let us compare these doctrines with the teaching
of Scripture:

The unregenerate man cannot believe the Gospel,
because it is foolishness to him; spiritual truths are spiritually discerned, and he lacks the requisite faculty, being
spiritually dead in trespasses and sins.[4]

It therefore follows that he must be born again (which
is the sovereign act of God) before he can repent and
believe. Faith in Christ is the gift of God. Thus salvation
is wholly of the Lord; he takes the initiative.[5]

There is no Gospel command in Scripture to believe
that Christ died for *your* sins. No-one can have legitimate

3. Mk. 10:17–22   4. 1 Cor. 1:18; 2:14; Eph. 2:1
5. Jn. 3:3–8; Phil. 1:6, 29; Jonah 2:9; 1 Pet. 1:2

assurance of this until he has been saved, and can make his 'calling and election sure' by wholehearted trust and obedience. Rather, the Gospel command is to repent and believe in Christ as the only Saviour, believing his promises and casting oneself on his mercy. We have already seen that Christ died for the elect (or, for those who believe).[6]

This modern gospel is presented with no hint that God is sovereign, and active in drawing to himself those whom he has chosen. But in Scripture these truths are not hidden lest they should cause offence; they are declared and even emphasized, since God is glorified when man can boast of nothing in himself to which salvation is due. 'I contribute nothing to my salvation except the sin from which I need to be saved.'[7]

It is implied that Christ's death merely made salvation *possible* for all, the salvation becoming actual only on the condition of belief. But the Scriptures without exception speak of Christ's death as actually effective in itself, because of its substitutionary nature, to redeem, reconcile, ransom, and save to the uttermost.[8]

Having examined this new gospel in its essentials, and shown that it is not the true Gospel of the Bible, we shall next show that its subsidiary terms are equally erroneous. We give a few examples of the sorts of points that are often made:

The sinner is appealed to as an honest seeker. 'Look into

6. Jn. 10:11–16; 15:13–14; Rom. 5:6–11; Eph. 5:25–27; Heb. 9:15
7. Acts 13:48; Mt. 11:25–30; Jn. 6:63–65; 15:16; Rom. 9:14–24; 1 Pet. 1:2
8. Rom. 5:10; 2 Cor. 5:21; Eph. 2:13; 1 Thess. 5:9–10; Heb. 10:10; 1 Pet. 1:18–20; 1 Jn. 4:10; Rev. 1:5

the evidence for yourself,' it is said, 'and you will be convinced. Tell God that you are honestly seeking him, and ask him to show himself to you.' Yet we are told in Scripture that no-one seeks after God; that no-one is honest before him; that the reaction of the unregenerate man is to flee from God's holiness because it shows up his own darkness.[9] It is a common experience that non-Christians who are put in this position, who are perhaps intellectually convinced of the truth of Christianity, *will not* 'commit themselves', or, if they do, often give no real evidence that there has been a supernatural change in their lives. Before a sinner is born again, he does not want to know the truth; he may show interest, even strong concern, in the Gospel, as his heart is prepared by the Holy Spirit, but he seeks as it were in spite of himself, always trying to hide from God.

Again, the benefits enjoyed by the Christian — joy, peace, fulfilment, meaning in life, etc. — are often made the ground of an appeal to the unsaved. This is, of course, a motive well-designed to lead the natural man to 'make a decision' for Christ. But it is misleading when divorced from the preaching of the wrath of God against sin, and the need for a complete change of nature, and the demand for true repentance, all of which are found in the New Testament Gospel.

Jesus is represented as a loving but impotent figure, standing and knocking, although he knows there is only one door-handle — on the inside, where the sinner alone can control it —; and the feeling excited is one of pity: 'He has done so much for you; will you not now open the door to him and allow him to bless you with his salvation?' This leads the hearer to feel that he has done God a fav-

9. Rom. 3:11; Jer. 17:9; Jn. 3:19

our by agreeing to believe. What could be more against the spirit of the tax-collector in the parable, who dared not approach God, but stood afar off, and cried in humility and repentance, 'God be merciful to me a sinner'?

This is what the modern gospel says; equally important is what it does *not* say. First, its preaching too often begins with man's problem, and works up to God's remedy, whereas Biblical preaching begins with the character of God – particularly with his holiness as set before us in the Law – and then shows that man's sin is the transgression of God's holy Law, for which God will condemn the sinner if he does not repent.[10] Jesus' answer to the rich young ruler who asked what he must do to inherit eternal life was: 'Thou knowest the commandments',[11] thus pointing him to the holiness of God in order to show him his sinfulness. This failure to preach God's Law, and the depth of man's sinfulness and guilt, is responsible for the evident lack of true conviction of sin in the souls of so many who profess conversion; and, furthermore, it leads sinners to believe that there is no need of a change of nature which it is not within their power to effect. 'To be incessantly telling a sinner to "come to Christ" is of little use, unless you tell him why he needs to come, and show him fully his sins' (J. C. Ryle). The modern evangelist often seems to proceed as if unaware of texts like 'Follow holiness, without which no man shall see the Lord'.[12]

Secondly, what the modern gospel *does* say about sin, repentance and faith, is too often a weakened version of what Scripture says. There is probably hardly a single

10. Gal. 3:10; Ezek. 18:4
11. Mk. 10:19   12. Heb. 12:14

person alive who would not be willing to 'admit his need'. But are we convinced that 'admitting one's need' is the same thing as the Biblical command: to repent of sin, to flee from it and abhor it? Does the invitation to admit one's need carry with it the urgency of the command of the apostles, prophets, and of the Lord himself, to repent? Does it lead sinners to *despair* of their natural ability, and to cast themselves on Christ for mercy? Furthermore, is all that is involved in faith, belief that Jesus Christ died for sinners? 'At this rate, the very devils are believers!' It is to be feared that many are taught to believe that they are saved, when in fact they are still in their sins.

Thirdly, is it wise to assert so positively how easy it is to become a Christian? It is doubtless true that the grace of God is free, yet Scripture exhorts men to *strive* to enter the Kingdom, to lay hold of God while he may be found, to examine their souls, and to seek the grace of God to repent of and forsake their sinful ways. Let it never be forgotten, however, that sinners *cannot* come to repentance and faith unless grace be given them by God; and one of the mischiefs of the modern evangelicalism is that it talks as if conversions could be manufactured at man's pleasure. Accordingly, as man is in full control, and it is all 'up to him', the modern system seeks to bring it within the power of all to be born again, merely by sincerely echoing the evangelist's closing prayer. Is not this the Romish doctrine of grace conferred '*ex opere operato*', mechanically, by the works of man? Have we forgotten that 'it is not of him that willeth, nor of him that runneth, but of God that hath mercy'?[13] Doubtless the rich young ruler was sincere in desiring eternal life, yet he

13. Rom. 9:16

went away unforgiven, because he was unwilling to turn from his sin.

What then is our conclusion? There is today, as there has been in other periods of history, a gospel which looks plausibly like the Biblical Gospel but which differs from it in several vital respects. We must give no place to this new teaching, but, like Paul, ensure that the truth of the Gospel continue with us.[14]

14. Gal. 2:5

7

OUR ATTITUDES

Ourselves

What is the effect of the Biblical Gospel upon the individual in living the Christian life? In this section, we wish to begin to answer this vital practical question. We shall not, however, be introspective in focusing attention on our individual spiritual lives, for our aim throughout is to turn attention away from what man does, and the position he takes, and look instead at who God is, and what he has done, does, and will do. From this, certain inferences about man's position and status will be obvious, and certain further things will be apparent about the nature of our responsibilities to other Christians and to the non-Christian world and individuals all around us. So, in this chapter, we are not in the least intending to be exhaustive, or even startlingly original. We merely wish to highlight a few points, in the hope that they will, first, show that the doctrine we hold is not conceived in the abstract alone, and divorced from practical experience; secondly, indicate some areas of experience where Christians are finding difficulty and where the doctrines we have outlined may show some solution; and thirdly, stimulate thought and prayer, and above all a God-centred life.

This last, indeed, is the crux of what we wish to say. 'Not I, but Christ,' wrote Paul.[1] We quote the whole passage, because it shows up a few of the basic weaknesses which result from some of the ideas that are currently in fashion: 'I have been crucified with Christ; it is no longer I who live, but Christ who lives in me; and the life I now

1. Gal. 2:20 ff.

live in the flesh I live by faith in the Son of God, who loved me and gave himself for me. I do not nullify the grace of God; for if justification were through the law, then Christ died to no purpose.' If only we all believed *that*, and lived by it! But, instead, we have slipped into the attitude that, really, our turning to God was rather a kind favour. We committed ourselves to him, as a recognition of some need in our lives, rather like one businessman doing a 50–50 deal with another: as a sort of gentleman's agreement, with both sides pleased and satisfied. Not so Paul! 'Crucified with Christ' – 'no longer I who live, but Christ' – Paul knew only too well that the Christian life does *not* consist of a man's going full steam ahead with good works for Christ. On the contrary, it is Christ who dwells within the heart of the man, providing the motive and power for all that he does. This is the crucial difference between the 'works' which Paul insists are not part of our salvation,[2] and those which James says are.[3] The former are the works which we misguidedly try to do to earn our fellowship with God, and the latter are those that proceed, as full day follows the dawn, from the indwelling and motivating Holy Spirit. It is only as we are found in Christ that we are able to do *anything* good at all.[4]

These are terrible and uncomfortable truths for us to stomach, for the obvious reason that, when we realize them fully, they make us feel small. But the fact that we find this to be so shows what we are stating all the time – and, alas, because we not only observe it in others but know it in ourselves – that we have far too high an opinion of ourselves. Humility is the quality we so often pray for and so earnestly wish was not required of us. Yet

2. Eph. 2:9   3. Jas. 2:24   4. Jn. 15:5

to realize, even in part, the amazing holiness of God, the horrible sinfulness of man, and then, the love that searched us out and *gave* us free pardon, life and glory can only make us grateful and thankful, breathlessly so. The reaction can*not* be: 'Well, having looked at all the evidence, and given the matter my sober and rational consideration, I will commit myself to this person who is being spoken of.' To state this – and it is not a caricature, so close is it to some current attitudes – is to reveal at once the arrogance and hardness which is contained in it. Let George Herbert present the opposite view in his poem *Love*:

Love bade me welcome: yet my soul drew back,
  Guiltie of dust and sinne.
But quick-ey'd Love, observing me grow slack
  From my first entrance in,
Drew nearer to me, sweetly questioning,
  If I lack'd any thing.

A guest, I answer'd, worthy to be here:
  Love said, You shall be he.
I, the unkinde, ungratefull? Ah my deare,
  I cannot look on thee.
Love took my hand, and smiling did reply,
  Who made the eyes but I?

Truth, Lord, but I have marr'd them: let my shame
  Go where it doth deserve.
And know you not, sayes Love, who bore the blame?
  My deare, then I will serve.
You must sit down, sayes Love, and taste my meat:
  So I did sit and eat.

[111]

When we realize our total debt to Christ thus, we shall again be on the joyful path the apostles took, a tiny group facing the world with the Gospel. We will join the reformers in their holy zeal, which led some even to the stake, and in their joy in holding to the truth. We will join those many faithful servants of the Master who have willingly given up comfort, prestige and security to go to the ends of the earth for the One who died for them. No sense of 50-50 partnership between Man and God: and little or nothing of the consequent lukewarm or self-induced 'spirituality' which is all too common today. If the Gospel were fully understood, who would ever worry whether 'commitment to Christ may mean I'll have to do a lot of things I may find uncomfortable'? If men and women realize that Christ has delivered their souls from death,[5] they will be able to continue, 'Shall he not also deliver our eyes from tears and our feet from falling?' These things are secondary: the need for salvation is, and should appear, so great that whatever service, whatever difficulties come with it should be lightly esteemed for 'the surpassing worth of knowing Christ Jesus my Lord'.[6] Indeed, as the rest of that passage shows, we should look at it the other way round, and count *all* things as loss for this, rejoicing rather to share suffering with Christ.

How far most of us seem from this ideal, which is the Biblical pattern, and the one which in every generation has marked out those Christians who live by the teaching of the Bible! Yet we are not so far off as to be unable to be drawn close. The remedy is clear from the principles we have already given. (Paul's teaching in his letter to the Philippians is especially relevant here.)

5. Ps. 116:8   6. Phil. 3:8

Finally, we are not left on our own with regard to the future. The partnership idea that we have been talking of, and which may be no stranger to many present-day Christians, results very easily in the man concerned looking at his future, 'thinking it all out for himself', settling it with himself whom he is to marry, what job he is to get, where he is to live, etc, and finally taking the attitude of – 'Well, this seems to be working out, therefore it must be the Lord's will.' If we believe Ephesians 2:8 and 9, let us also rejoice in verse 10: 'For by grace you have been saved through faith; and this is not your own doing, it is the gift of God – not because of works, lest any man should boast. For we are his workmanship, created in Christ Jesus for good works, which God prepared beforehand, that we should walk in them.' The application is obvious, though it is very wide: it covers the largest areas of life and the smallest too. 'You are not your own; you were bought with a price.'[7] This whole subject is beyond our present scope, and we content ourselves with a reference to the Bibliography for further reading on these and related topics. We mention it in outline, however, to show that in this area too there is a need for the re-vitalizing which a fresh and right awareness of God's sovereignty will give. It will have application in the areas of personal devotional life and behaviour, and in corporate Christianity. It will take effect in a man's vocation and whole life-work. We ourselves, however, are so conscious of the need to apply these truths in our own lives that we hesitate to advise others in detail. Yet with the foundation right, we are confident that the whole building will develop as the Lord wills it to do: 'you are God's field, God's building'.[8]

7. 1 Cor. 6:19–20   8. 1 Cor. 3:9

Other Christians

The fact of God's great love, free and undeserved, has very definite application in our relationships with others. One of the classic Biblical expressions of this is found in 1 John 4, verses 7 to 12: 'Beloved, let us love one another; for love is of God, and he who loves is born of God, and knows God. He who does not love does not know God: for God is love. In this the love of God was made manifest among us, that God sent his only Son into the world, so that we might live through him. In this is love, not that we loved God, but that he loved us, and sent his Son to be the propitiation for our sins. Beloved, if God so loved us, we also ought to love one another. No man has ever seen God; if we love one another, God abides in us and his love is perfected in us.'

This passage shows quite clearly the chain of reasoning required. God has loved us without our deserving it: when, therefore, he 'comes and makes his abode with us',[9] it must follow that we love one another. We assent to this, for sure. Yet that our love to one another is in fact often cold and at best spasmodic is all too clear from experience. With the passage from John's epistle in mind, we find ourselves asking whether we fail because we have lost sight of the great love wherewith *God first loved us.*[10] Let us again see our unworthiness, and God's free love, and we shall be on the road to loving one another 'in deed and truth, and not in word only'.[11]

Another basic application of the Gospel of grace is the need for humility. We all know of this, and acknowledge our lack of it, and yet we perhaps aim at it in the wrong way. We approach it sometimes as if it were something

9. Jn. 14:23   10. Eph. 2:4   11. 1 Jn. 3:18

we achieved. 'Humility and how I achieved it.' We have to learn that humility is the state of realizing that we *are* nothing and can *do* nothing by ourselves that will be of any good at all. As that realization is one of the basic presuppositions of the whole Gospel of grace, can it be that our own lack of humility again underlies the fact that we are in danger of losing sight of precisely this Gospel? Humility is the state of a man who realizes that he is not just inadequate for life, or restless, or purposeless, but totally sinful and unworthy, and who realizes his dependence on God for everything. If we realize afresh all that was done for our salvation,[12] can we *not* be humbled? We enter the state of humility through the door of humiliation – and it is, alas, to this that we put up some of our strongest, most foolish and most obstinate barriers.

We now turn to apply what has been said to communal Christian living, doing so in terms of general principles deduced from Scripture.

First, then, we are to live in loving fellowship with one another. On what is this based? Note, first, on what it is *not* based. It cannot and must not rest on any foundation of common culture or race, intellectual or social background, or any such human basis. It is to our shame that so much that passes today for Christian fellowship is, in fact, a happy concursus of people on one or other of these bases. Observe the effect when the Christian enters who does not share it. That this is doomed from the start should be obvious from the fact that it is, like the theology about which we are expressing concern, man-centred, and shows all the fruits of this basic misconception. Lack of love, of sympathy, of openness and honesty

12. See especially Phil. 2:1–11

[115]

in a fellowship, and the presence of petty squabbling and bickering, are all tell-tale symptoms of the basic man-centredness of much that passes for fellowship today.

What, then, is our basis to be? Surely, the things all Christians have in common: their awareness of their own worthlessness, their having been snatched out of the fire by a loving heavenly Father; their participation in the Holy Spirit; their organic membership of the Body of Christ in their new status as children of God; and their common heritage as heirs of eternal life and glory.[13] Of these points one in particular is vital for a true understanding of the *basis* of fellowship: we refer to the organic membership of the Body of Christ. As family love, ideally, exists between those who share common parentage, so Christian love should be in evidence between those who are brothers and sisters as children of God. Thus love is not just 'the best way of living together, for the sake of peace and quiet'; it is the characteristic state of the Family of God, who is himself love in all its fulness.

It would be a long task (though a thrilling one) to describe how this works out in practice; but it would be presumptuous for us to attempt it. 1 Corinthians chapter 13 is an excellent starting-point, and most of us would find that verses 4 to 7 set a very high standard if we determined to put into practice all that these four verses contain:

> *Love is patient and kind*
> *it is not jealous or boastful*
> *it is not arrogant or rude*

13. Zech. 3:2; Phil. 2:1; 1 Cor. 12:12; Rom. 8:16; Tit. 3:7

Love does not insist on its own way
it is not irritable or resentful
it does not rejoice at wrong
but rejoices in the right
Love bears all things
believes all things
hopes all things
endures all things.

Our lives must become a visible exposition of these principles, as we walk together in the light,[14] open and honest with one another, and praying for each other in all these things – for exhortation without prayer will of itself prove to be of little spiritual value.

Finally, what is fellowship aiming at? We begin with its secondary purpose. True fellowship will be of great value in personal comfort, encouragement, and strength to all that belong to it. If one member suffers, what do the others do?[15] Do they pretend they have not noticed, and show their embarrassment in silence? Surely, they suffer together, and weep with those that weep as much as they rejoice with those that rejoice.[16] As we remind ourselves of the example of the early Church,[17] the contrast with our own attitude becomes uncomfortably apparent. It is all too easy for western Christians to live in luxury, hardly giving a thought for their brethren suffering for the faith in Soviet prisons and in other ways. This principle is as wide as the world in application, and as minute in detail as a fellowship of 'two or three'. Let us practise it, and rejoice so to do.

If this is the secondary purpose of our fellowship, what

14. See 1 Jn. 1   15. 1 Cor. 12:26   16. Rom. 12:15
17. Acts 4:32–35

is the main purpose of our love? Christ said 'By this shall all men know that ye are my disciples, if ye have love one to another.'[18] What a challenge, and responsibility! The warmth of a genuine Christian fellowship is one of the most attractive things in the world, beyond the charm of the individual personality or the fascinating depths of intellectual discussion. Let us test ourselves: would the outsider, stumbling upon a group Bible Study, appreciate that he had come face to face with people who loved each other in deed and in truth?[19] Or would he find a group of individuals determined to express their points of view, to win arguments, to hold supposed truth and forget love? We are none of us guiltless, and no stones are cast. But that is no reason for not attempting to put right things that are wrong.

Love is, evidently, above all things a quality which exhortation can do precious little to produce. Which is just as well! We must again come to the Lord and Giver of life and confess that we are incapable of it ourselves. Then, as we seek him in prayer, and in his Word and sacraments, and as he richly pours out his Spirit upon us, we shall begin to find the fruits of the Spirit becoming apparent – like the wind, without visible starting-point – and the first of these fruits is the amazing and treasured love that we long to see more and more in ourselves and in the Body of Christ throughout the world. Once again, we are powerless. Let us then turn to him who is Power and Love, and seek in him all we lack.

Evangelism

The Lord has declared his will to man in the Holy Scriptures, and the central message of the Scriptures is

18. Jn. 13:35   19. 1 Jn. 3:18

the Gospel. We have seen what that Gospel is: it is the good news of salvation by grace, for the Lord Jesus Christ has redeemed his people. But the Church of Jesus Christ has been entrusted with this glorious good news; and we are not to keep it to ourselves — we have also been given the task of evangelism, which is simply to declare the Gospel to the world. Just as God has given the good news to us, we are to pass it on to others; for this is God's means of bringing men and women to salvation — through the preaching and hearing of the Gospel.

Evangelism is not a making of proselytes; it is not persuading people to make a decision; it is not proving that God exists, or making out a good case for the truth of Christianity; it is not inviting someone to a meeting; it is not exposing the contemporary dilemma, or arousing interest in Christianity; it is not wearing a badge saying 'Jesus Saves'! Some of these things are right and good in their place, but none of them should be confused with evangelism. To evangelize is to declare on the authority of God what he has done to save sinners, to warn men of their lost condition, to direct them to repent, and to believe on the Lord Jesus Christ. Richard Baxter gives some valuable directions for this task:

'We must take all opportunities we possibly can to instruct them how to attain salvation. If the person be ignorant, labour to make him understand the chief happiness of man, how far he was once possessed of it; the covenant God then made with him; how he broke it; what penalty he incurred; and what misery he brought himself into: teach him his need of a Redeemer; how Christ did mercifully interpose, and bear the penalty; what the new covenant is; how men are drawn to Christ; and what are the riches and privileges which believers have in him. If he is not moved by these things, then show him the excellency of the glory he neglects; the extremity and eternity of the torments of the damned; the justice of enduring them for wilfully refusing grace; the certainty, nearness, and terrors of death and judgement; the vanity of all things below; the sinfulness of sin; the preciousness of Christ; the necessity of regeneration, faith, and holiness, and the true nature of them. If, after all, you find him entertaining false hopes, then urge him to examine his state; show him the necessity of doing so; help him in it; nor leave him till you have convinced him of his misery and remedy. Show him how vain and destructive it is to join Christ and his duties, to compose his justifying righteousness. Yet be sure to draw him to the use of all means; such as hearing and reading the Word, calling upon God, and associating with the godly; persuade him to forsake sin, avoid all temptations to sin, especially evil companions, and to wait patiently on God in the use of means, as the way in which God will be found.'

Our motives for evangelism are important, for unless they are Scriptural motives, our evangelism may become distorted or cold, and God will not honour a self-centred evangelist.

Very dangerous and subtle are false motives, and liable to deceive ourselves as well as others. It is all too possible for selfishness to be the driving force. One may evangelize in order to boost his self-esteem by 'bringing someone through', as the phrase goes, or in order spiritually to keep up with the Joneses, or to feel important in the service of God. We need to examine ourselves concerning these matters in the light of God's Word, and to repent, and to come to him for cleansing.

Having said this, we allow that there is a right form of self-love which is a legitimate motive for evangelism. This is a yielding to an inner compulsion to evangelize, a compulsion which is the work of the Holy Spirit, and which gives no rest until it is obeyed. For one's own happiness and peace of mind, it is right to follow such a compulsion – as Paul found: 'For though I preach the gospel, I have nothing to glory of: for necessity is laid upon me; yea, woe is unto me, if I preach not the gospel! For if I do this thing willingly, I have a reward: but if against my will, a dispensation of the gospel is committed unto me.'[20]

But a higher motive than this, and a necessary one, is love for the lost to whom one declares the good news. Love seeks the best for the beloved; if we know the value of the Gospel of salvation which we possess, this treasure in earthen vessels,[21] then it is the act of love to declare it to the lost around us. If the Lord Jesus Christ is really to us the One whom our souls love, the chiefest among ten thousand, then how are we to fulfil our duty to love our neighbours as ourselves, unless we tell them of him? If we look upon the lost with the same compassion as our Saviour, we shall be driven to help them – to tell them the Gospel by which they can be delivered from their terrible plight. 'But when he saw the multitudes, he was moved with compassion on them, because they fainted, and were scattered abroad, as sheep having no shepherd.'[22]

The highest motive of all is love for the Lord himself. Without this, all else is vain. To love God is the first commandment, and the highest and most awesome privilege. How gracious he is, that he has made us able to love him, because he first loved us![23] And John also says, as

20. 1 Cor. 9:16–17; cf. Jer. 20:9   21. 2 Cor. 4:7
22. Mt. 9:36   23. 1 Jn. 4:19

did the Lord Jesus himself, 'For this is the love of God, that we keep his commandments: and his commandments are not grievous.'[24] We have a commandment, a Great Commission, from the Lord; we show our love to him by our obedience: 'Go ye into all the world, and preach the gospel to every creature.'[25] It has been well said that the sovereignty of God is expressed in his commands as much as in his decrees. Because he is our Sovereign Lord, when he commands, we are to obey. And if we love him, we *want* to obey: we shall be concerned that he should be glorified, that his will should be done. The Christian who loves his Lord rejoices with the angels in heaven over each sinner who repents, and gives praise to the God of all grace.

Love for God is the only sufficient motive for evangelism. Self-love will give way to self-centredness; love for the lost will fail with those whom we cannot love, and when difficulties seem unsurmountable. Only a deep love for God will keep us following his way, declaring his Gospel, when human resources fail. Only our love for God – and, more important, his love for us – will keep us from the dangers which beset us. When the desire for popularity with men, or for success in human terms, tempts us to water down the Gospel, to make it palatable, then only if we love God will we stand fast by his truth and his ways.

We turn to the question of the results of evangelism. Preaching the Gospel is not an end in itself: it is the means God has appointed for the salvation of souls, and so the evangelist expects, and ought to expect, that his work will lead to conversions. But here is where a full realiza-

24. 1 Jn. 5:3; cf. Jn. 14:15   25. Mk. 16:15

tion of the sovereignty of God in salvation is so essential for the evangelist, to keep him from pride, and in humble reliance on the Lord alone. Thus it was that Paul could say to the Corinthians: 'Who then is Paul, and who is Apollos, but ministers by whom ye believed, even as the Lord gave to every man? I have planted, Apollos watered; but God gave the increase. So then neither is he that planteth any thing, neither he that watereth; but God that giveth the increase.'[26]

Such a reliance will lead us to admit that in ourselves we are quite unfitted for the work of evangelism, for it is a spiritual work. Praise God, the implanting of new life is his work, and even our part is done through him alone. 'Not that we are sufficient of ourselves to think any thing as of ourselves; but our sufficiency is of God; who also hath made us able ministers of the new testament; not of the letter, but of the Spirit: for the letter killeth, but the Spirit giveth life.'[27]

God's sovereign rule is not only the source of our ability, but also the ground of our confidence. How a knowledge of this fact should comfort and strengthen us! When Paul was in Corinth, he was afraid, because of the opposition of the Jews, but God said to him, 'Be not afraid, but speak, and hold not thy peace: for I am with thee, and no man shall set on thee to hurt thee: for I have much people in this city.'[28] God will gather in his elect, and no opposition of men or Satan shall prevail against his almighty power. He is 'the Lord of the harvest',[29] to whom alone we should look in prayer and in action. When we proclaim the Gospel, we proclaim the Word of the Lord; and that Word, as it is applied by the

26. 1 Cor. 3:5–7   27. 2 Cor. 3:5–6   28. Acts 18:9–10
29. Mt. 9:36–38

Holy Spirit to the hearts of men, has great power. So Peter says: those who have been saved are 'born again, not of corruptible seed, but of incorruptible, by the word of God, which liveth and abideth for ever'.[30]

If, as we have seen, salvation is not of the free-will of man, but of God, it follows that the results of evangelism are entirely from the Lord's hand, and according to his will. Therefore we should not be surprised when some hear and accept the Gospel, while others reject it. God has promised (and his promises are sure): 'For as the rain cometh down, and the snow from heaven, and returneth not thither, but watereth the earth, and maketh it bring forth and bud, that it may give seed to the sower, and bread to the eater: so shall my word be that goeth forth out of my mouth: it shall not return unto me void, but it shall accomplish that which I please, and it shall prosper in the thing whereto I sent it.'[31] These words indicate that God's Word does exactly what he has decreed: nothing more, nothing less. When a group of people hear the Gospel, those whom it pleases God to call at that time, believe, having been elected unto salvation; those whom God passes over and rejects, harden their hearts against the Gospel, and are confirmed in their sinful rebellion. So the ministers of the Gospel are 'unto God a sweet savour of Christ, in them that are saved, and in them that perish: To the one we are the savour of death unto death; and to the other the savour of life unto life. And who is sufficient for these things?'[32] We are awed to think that every presentation of the Gospel has such a spiritual and eternal effect on the souls of all those who hear: unto death, or unto life.

It is, of course, true that some who are awakened under

30. 1 Pet. 1:23   31. Is. 55:10–11   32. 2 Cor. 2:15–16

Gospel preaching afterwards go back, and a consideration of the results of evangelism would be incomplete without facing the question of the genuineness of those results. We must sadly conclude, from Scripture and from experience, that not all who at first appear to be saved are truly born again. 'Our Lord's parable of the sower implies that, however good the seed might be, and careful the sower, there would be stony-ground hearers, and thorny-ground hearers, going a certain length and then turning back. So the backslidings complained of are such as the apostles experienced, and such as our Lord led us to anticipate under the preaching of his own full gospel' (H. Bonar). So, if some supposed converts prove not to be genuine, the preacher is not necessarily at all to be blamed; though this provides no excuse for preaching in such a way as to encourage false professions.

In the light of all that has been said, what should be our methods of evangelism? Here, as in all things, our only rule and guide must be the Holy Scriptures. No pragmatic justification is valid before God; but 'the just shall live by faith'.

First, and perhaps self-evidently, our evangelism should be an accurate presentation of the true Gospel. It should be complete; it should be balanced – every point given the same emphasis and importance that Scripture gives it; and it should be free from errors. We must not hide the unpalatable parts of the Gospel, such as the wrath of God against sin. Such truth always arouses opposition, but God can remove it. Nor ought we to imply (perhaps without stating it explicitly) that salvation is a matter of man's free-will. Like Paul, let us renounce 'the hidden things of dishonesty, not walking in craftiness, nor handling the word of God deceitfully; but by manifestation of the truth commending ourselves to every man's conscience in the sight of God.'[33]

Secondly, our evangelism should be openly grounded in the Bible. It is quite possible to present an accurate summary of the Gospel in one's own words. But how much more honouring to God, how much more effective, to show directly from the Bible that these things are not the opinions of men, but the authoritative declarations of God. 'For the word of God is quick, and powerful, and sharper than any two-edged sword, piercing even to the dividing asunder of soul and spirit, and of the joints and marrow, and is a discerner of the thoughts and intents of the heart.'[34]

Thirdly, the non-essentials should not detract from the essentials. There are many forms of communication which can be used today; most of these are quite unobjectionable in themselves, but there is in many cases a danger of the real Gospel message becoming lost in the trimmings. This can be so with Christian songs, or some Christian radio programmes, or attempts to give a Christian analysis of modern culture, etc.

Fourthly, we must never forget that preaching the Gospel is communication with real people, and that their individual characteristics must be taken into account. Thus the preacher will adapt his vocabulary and style (though not the basic content of what he says) to his audience; and the missionary will live with the people of the country to which he goes, as far as possible adopting their way of life, and removing unnecessary cultural barriers.

Let us take a brief survey of various kinds of evangelism, and apply to them some of these principles.

33. 2 Cor. 4:2   34. Heb. 4:12

The evangelism which is most familiar to many Christians is the preaching of the Gospel in an evangelistic meeting – whether a church service, or a Christian Union meeting, or an open-air meeting, or a vast 'crusade' meeting. These provide opportunities for many non-Christians at one time to hear the Gospel, in conditions ideal to gain their full attention to what is said, and with the possibility afterwards to discuss the message with Christians who are present. However, there are dangers which must be avoided: the preacher may easily draw attention to himself rather than to Christ; he may do almost irremediable harm by misleading statements or emphases, or by emotional 'decisionism', which encourages professions of faith from those in whose hearts there is no saving grace at work. The Lord's name may even be dishonoured by anecdotes which are inappropriate to the Gospel. Evangelistic meetings themselves, of course, do not necessarily involve these dangers; they are abuses which ought to be guarded against, while every opportunity of thus benefiting the souls of men should be seized.

'They that were scattered abroad went every where preaching the word.'[35] There is a great need in these days for ordinary Christians to regain this ministry of the early church – every believer an evangelist. Let us be found faithful servants in thus spreading the Word of Christ. If we know and love the Lord, let us also have a thorough knowledge of the Gospel, and prayerfully seek as he gives the opportunities to tell our friends and acquaintances of him. Here the keynotes should be simplicity, spontaneity, and sincerity. A testimony which is Christ-centred and not self-centred can also be very

35. Acts 8:4

[127]

valuable: 'Come and hear, all ye that fear God, and I will declare what he hath done for my soul.'[36] A true and up-to-date testimony will often strike home to the heart. In conversations with his friends, a Christian may be able to sort out problems, to make the Gospel quite clear, and to be a true ambassador for Christ. We must, of course, avoid any pressurizing, or fruitless argument or persuasion. But as the Holy Spirit leads and enables us, God can use us in this way.

When Luther was imprisoned in the Wartburg, he was given by the Lord the task of translating the Bible into his native German. Dr. Merle d'Aubigné comments: 'The reform was no longer in the hand of the reformer. The Bible was brought forward, and Luther withdrew. God shews himself, and man disappears. The reformer has intrusted the *Book* to the hands of his contemporaries, and each person is now enabled to understand and listen to God himself.' It is no less true today that the Gospel in printed form can be a very effective means of evangelism, and we have a duty and an opportunity to distribute portions of Scripture, and all forms of Christian literature true to the Word of God.

We must not leave the subject of evangelism without speaking of missionary work. Perhaps our greatest need is a combination of a local with a world-wide vision of God's work. The commission for evangelism is world-wide; for the Church of Jesus Christ is composed of his elect and redeemed people from all nations, and kindreds, and people, and tongues.[37] The Gospel is to be preached in all the world for a witness to all nations, and then the end shall come.[38] How concerned we should be, therefore, to take part by prayer and giving in this great work

36. Ps. 66:16   37. Rev. 7:9   38. Mt. 24:14

of God – and, if the Lord calls us, to go as missionaries ourselves.

Perhaps the reader feels, as the writers certainly do, 'Who is sufficient for these things?' It is here that the Scriptures give their sweetest comfort and strongest encouragement: it is not as of ourselves, weak, sinful, rebellious, foolish; but as of God, sovereign, almighty, holy, the ruler of all, that we are to preach the Gospel. Christ said: 'All power [authority] is given unto me in heaven and in earth. *Go ye therefore* . . .'[39] Paul could say, 'I can do all things through Christ which strengtheneth me.'[40] Saved and equipped for service by grace, through faith, let us take God at his word, and go forward for him and with him.

But as we were allowed of God to be put in trust with the gospel, even so we speak; not as pleasing men, but God, which trieth our hearts.

39. Mt. 28:18   40. Phil. 4:13

8

THE END OF THE GOSPEL: WORSHIP

To the question, 'What is the chief end of man?', the Westminster Shorter Catechism gives the famous answer: 'Man's chief end is to glorify God, and to enjoy him for ever.' To this simple but profound statement our hearts, renewed by the Spirit of the living God, utter a heartfelt amen. Something within us tells us that this rings true; this, pre-eminently, is the purpose for which God intended man — a purpose which can now be realized, as a result of the saving work of the Lord Jesus Christ for us.

In these pages, we have endeavoured to set out what we believe to be the doctrines of the Gospel of the grace of God, revealed in the Scriptures. But merely to believe in our minds that these doctrines are true is to profess a form of godliness, without power. There are, we must sadly admit, those who would agree fully with the doctrinal position embodied in the earlier chapters, and yet whose hearts are cold toward the Lord Jesus; whose churches are devoid of the presence of the Holy Spirit, the Lord and Giver of life; whose preaching is but philosophical lecturing. With those who say that such people, for all their 'soundness', have understood the *letter* only, and not the *spirit*, of the Gospel, we wholeheartedly agree. As Joseph Hart wrote:

> *True religion's more than notion;*
> *Something must be known and felt.*

So we ask this question: how ought an understanding of the doctrines of grace to affect our attitude to God? What will be the effect upon our relationship with our God of the application by the Holy Spirit to our innermost being of these doctrines, and of their being written with letters of fire upon the tables of our hearts?

The effect upon us ought surely to be that we see ourselves as we are – DEBTORS. Debtors to the infinite mercy and grace of the God who has wonderfully delivered us. We acknowledge, upon being asked 'How much owest thou unto my Lord?',[1] that we owe everything to him. All our fountains are in Zion, the City of God, of which, by grace, we have been made members – and in the Lord Jesus Christ, who is King in Zion, and who has become our own King and Lord. Day by day, as we walk along the path foreordained, as we look back and see how all things have worked together for our good, we become more and more aware of *how much* we owe; but not until the great day when, before the throne of God, we worship in the company of the innumerable hosts of angels, of the Church of the first-born enrolled in heaven, of the spirits of just men made perfect, and of Jesus himself, the mediator of the new covenant – not until then shall we fully realize the breadth and length and height and depth of God's love toward us:

> *When I stand before the throne,*
> *Dressed in beauty not my own;*
> *When I see Thee as Thou art,*
> *Love Thee with unsinning heart;*
> *Then, Lord, shall I fully know,*
> *Not till then, how much I owe.*

As we raise, with Samuel, our Ebenezers,[2] we find our hearts exclaiming in love and wonder: 'Oh, to grace how

1. Lk. 16:5   2. 1 Sam. 7:12

[131]

great a debtor daily I'm constrained to be.' This is where
a right relationship with God begins; it begins with the
realization of our debt to his amazing grace.

There are many basic things that characterize the
relationship with God of one who possesses a deep experi-
mental knowledge of the doctrines of the Gospel. Let us
touch on a few of them.

First, and foremost: *he will be a worshipper*. Was it not
in order that he might be worshipped that God made
man? And when man fell, was it not in order that this
purpose might yet be fulfilled that he saved man? The
Gospel makes rebels into worshippers; those who once
were afar off, enemies of God, have, by the blood of
Christ, been brought into the very presence of the King
of kings and Lord of lords in order to worship him. 'Tell
it out among the heathen that the Lord is King!' cries the
Psalmist in Psalm 96 – and the response he seeks amongst
those who hear this message is that they should bow down
before his footstool, worshipping the Lord in the beauty
of holiness.[3] This is giving God the glory due unto his
name. If God is King in Zion, and we are citizens of the
heavenly Jerusalem, then nothing less than perfect
submission, and the worship of our hearts, is what God
requires of us, and what he delights to see. But God not
only requires worship of us – he has, in his mercy, made
us *fit* to worship him, having, as it were, mended and
returned our broken and rusted harps, making them even
more harmonious and brilliant than they were before
they were (so it seemed) irretrievably battered by the
fall – in order that we might sing the new song of the
redeemed people of God.[4]

3. Ps. 96:9   4. Rev. 5:9

Furthermore, *his worship is a continuing activity*. It begins here below when the burden of his sins is removed; it continues in glory, as, perfected in the Lord Jesus Christ, he casts his crown before the great white throne upon which he sees the One whom, previously, he had loved, having not seen. The Christian who is a worshipper will — may we say it? — be immediately 'at home' when he arrives at the end of his pilgrimage, heaven itself — for heaven, the place where the worship of God is unceasing, is a prepared place for a prepared people — those who, by the working of the Holy Spirit in their lives, are being made ready to enter it.

What a change would be effected in our own lives, and in our Christian Unions and Churches, if only we learned what worshipping in spirit and in truth meant! We speak glibly of 'joy' in the Christian life; but is it the joy of the Psalmist who spoke from experience when he said 'In thy presence is fulness of joy; in thy right hand there are pleasures for evermore',[5] because he had learned to worship? Do we say, with longing in our hearts: 'Blessed are they that dwell in thy house: they will be still praising thee'?[6] Do we know what it is to worship night and day as Anna delighted to do?[7] Many times we read in Scripture of those who could say, with Simeon: 'Mine eyes have seen thy salvation',[8] and who, with thankful hearts, *worshipped* — yet how little we know of the joy of such worship ourselves! How important it is that we, for whom so much has been done in salvation, should learn again to bow down before Almighty God, glorifying God in worshipping him; finding, as we do so, that to worship God is the means by which we enjoy him!

Let us, then, rid ourselves of the idea that Christians

5. Ps. 16:11   6. Ps. 84:4   7. Lk. 2:36–38   8. Lk. 2:30

should first and foremost be *workers*, and teach the newly converted to become habitual *worshippers*. We need not fear that to do this will result in a lack of evangelism; far from it! A group of worshippers will also be a group of powerful witnesses to the grace of God; these are the Christians whose testimonies convict unbelievers, for they are able, from the heart, to say; 'Come near, and hear what God hath done for my soul.' Gone will be those barren and sad prayer-meetings, so often little more than the repetition, in shopping-list fashion, of 'prayer-needs', and gone will be the supposition that prayer must always be *for* this or that; gone, too, will be the subconscious attitude which encourages Christians to put more faith in the power of prayer than in the one who is the inspirer and hearer of all true prayer. Instead, times of prayer will be times of worship, times when the presence of the Holy Spirit is longed for and sought after; times when we pour out our souls before God, and bring before him, in intercessory prayer, those things for which he himself has laid a burden on our hearts. 'Whom have I in heaven but thee? And there is none upon earth that I desire beside thee'.[9] Let us learn to pray like this, and we shall find to our joy that God will delight to pour down upon us showers of blessing; we shall begin to *prove* the power of prayer, for

> *Prayer makes the darkened cloud withdraw,*
> *Prayer climbs the ladder Jacob saw,*
> *Gives exercise to faith and love,*
> *Brings every blessing from above.*

How much we need to ask the Lord, as did his disciples, to teach us to pray![10]

9. Ps. 73:25   10. Lk. 11:1

Intimately bound up with this are three further attitudes which constitute a close walk with God – which, indeed, could be said to constitute the worship of our lives: *love of God*, *fear of God* and *obedience to his Law*. Deuteronomy 10:12–22 sets out wonderfully what it is that God requires of those upon whom he has set his love: it is 'to fear the Lord thy God, to walk in all his ways, and to love him, and to serve the Lord thy God with all thy heart and with all thy soul, to keep the commandments of the Lord, and his statutes, which I command thee this day for thy good'. Here is a picture of the normal Christian life, as far as the Christian's relationship with God is concerned. For it is as we realize in our hearts that the God unto whom 'belongeth the heaven, and the heaven of heavens, the earth, with all that therein is', had a delight in us sinners, to choose us out of all peoples, that we might be to him a people for his own possession, that we respond to him in love and adoration, that we learn to fear him, and consequently to obey him.

There is so much superficiality among us today, so much 'smooth and fair speech', that it is significant that the Scriptural expression 'a God-fearing man' has almost entirely dropped out of use. Would we (to take a small but significant example) sing hymns of praise to the Lord with our hands in our pockets if we really knew something of the sovereignty, majesty and holiness of God? Why is so much devotional preaching and writing today oriented toward the man-centred sort of question that begins: 'How can I . . .?'? We would suggest that these things are indications of something radically wrong with much present-day piety, indications that we have not 'seen the Lord, high and lifted up', but only a pale shadow. Once let us become God-centred in our thinking, treating the things of God with the seriousness they deserve, calling Jesus 'Lord, Lord' *and* doing the things he says, 'working out our salvation with fear and trembling', and we shall find that he will visit us, individually and corporately, working within us that which will please him.

Finally, the Christian in close communion with his Lord will *await his coming*, for 'the grace of God hath appeared, bringing salvation to all men, instructing us, to the intent that, denying ungodliness and worldly lusts, we should live soberly and righteously and godly in this present world, looking for the blessed hope and appearing of the glory of our great God and Saviour Jesus Christ.'[11] This hope of the appearing of the Lord Jesus Christ, and of being with him in eternity with that multitude which no man can number, who have washed their robes in his blood, is what gives him courage on this earth; for he knows that this life is but a pilgrimage, a journey in a foreign land. Soon he will be going home to that heavenly country of which he is a citizen.[12] It is often said of Christians that they are 'so heavenly minded that they are no earthly use'. The truth is that the *more* heavenly minded the Christian is (and he is commanded to set his mind on things that are above[13]), the *more* he will be the salt of the earth and the light of the world, as he seeks to be. Let us meditate often upon heaven, longing, with Paul, to depart to be with Christ, awaiting in joyful anticipation the time when God will call us to enter into the 'Sabbath rest that remaineth for the people of God'. Let us fulfil our calling in this world, wherever God would have us be, whatever he would have us do, in the

11. Tit. 2:11–13
12. Phil. 3:20; Heb. 11:13–16   13. Col. 3:1–4

light of eternity, seeking to be found, when the Lord comes again, as profitable servants, working faithfully for him. And then, in that great day, when the books are opened, and the secrets of all hearts revealed, the Lord Jesus Christ, our incomparable Saviour whom we shall see face to face in all his beauty and glory, will call us with those wonderful and precious words: 'Well done, thou good and faithful servant; enter thou into the joy of thy Lord.'

Make a joyful noise before the King, the Lord; for he cometh to judge the earth.

Bibliography

An asterisk denotes a work of particular value as an introduction to the subject.

DOCTRINAL

Boettner, Loraine, *The Reformed Doctrine of Predestination* (Eerdmans)

*Bonar, Horatius, *God's Way of Holiness* (MP)

*Douglas, J. D. (Ed.), *New Bible Dictionary* (IVP) (articles on covenant, prayer, providence, election, predestination, sanctification)

Edwards, Jonathan, *An Essay on the Freedom of the Will* (Yale)

Hodge, Charles, *Systematic Theology* (JC)

Luther, Martin, *The Bondage of the Will* (JC)

*Machen, J. G., *The Christian View of Man* (BT)

Murray, John, *Exposition of Romans* (MMS)

*Murray, John, *Redemption Accomplished and Applied* (BT)

Owen, John, *The Death of Death in the Death of Christ* (BT; *Works*, Vol 10)

*Pink, A. W., *The Sovereignty of God* (BT)

Tasker, R. V. G., *The Biblical Doctrine of the Wrath of God* (TP)

*Warfield, B. B., *God's Immeasurable Love* (in *Biblical and Theological Studies*, PRPC)

Westminster Assembly, *The Confession of Faith, &c* (Free Presbyterian Church of Scotland)

DEVOTIONAL AND EVANGELISTIC

Alleine, Joseph, *Alarm to the Unconverted* (BT)

Baxter, Richard, *The Saints' Everlasting Rest* (Associated Publishers and Authors Inc.)

*Blanchard, J., *Right with God* (BT)
*Bonar, Horatius, *God's Way of Peace* (EP)
 Bunyan, John, *Prayer* (BT)
 Flavel, John, *Mystery of Providence* (BT)
*France, R. T., *The Living God* (IVP)
*Griffiths, Michael, *Take My Life* (IVP)
*Hallesby, O., *Prayer* (IVP)
*Hession, Roy, *We would see Jesus* (CLC)
 Hodge, Charles, *The Way of Life* (BT)
*Lloyd-Jones, D. Martyn, *The Plight of Man and the Power of God* (PI)
*Lloyd-Jones, D. Martyn, *Truth Unchanged, Unchanging* (EP)
*Newton, John, *Letters* (BT)
*Ryle, J. C., *Holiness* (JC)

PRACTICAL

*Chantry, Walter, *Today's Gospel – Authentic or Synthetic?* (BT)
 Kuyper, Abraham, *Lectures on Calvinism* (Eerdmans)
 Lloyd-Jones, D. Martyn, *Preaching & Preachers* (HS)
*Murray, Iain, *The Forgotten Spurgeon* (BT)
*Packer, J. I., *Evangelism and the Sovereignty of God* (IVP)
*Packer, J. I., Introduction to John Owen's *Death of Death* (BT)
*Stott, J. R. W., *Our Guilty Silence* (HS)

HISTORICAL AND BIOGRAPHICAL

*Cadier, Jean, *Calvin – The Man God Mastered* (IVP)
 Cunningham, William, *The Reformers and the Theology of the Reformation* (BT)
 Dallimore, A., *George Whitefield* (BT)
 D'Aubigné, J. H. Merle, *History of the Reformation* (various portions reprinted by BT under title *The Reformation in England*)

*Ryle, J. C., *The Christian Leaders of the Last Century* (selected papers reprinted by BT under the title *Five Christian Leaders*)

*Toplady, Augustus, *Diary and Selection of Hymns* (Gospel Standard Baptist Trust)

Key to publishers

BT – Banner of Truth Trust; CLC – Christian Literature Crusade; EP – Evangelical Press; HS – Hodder and Stoughton; IVP – Inter-Varsity Press; JC – James Clarke; MMS – Marshall, Morgan and Scott; MP – Moody Press; PI – Pickering and Inglis; PRPC – Presbyterian and Reformed Publishing Company; TP – Tyndale Press.